PRAISE FOR

Ageless Entrepreneur

"Entrepreneurship is not just for the young. It is a mindset, and it's never too late to take charge of your life and become an entrepreneur. That's Fred Dawkins's message in a nutshell, and nobody tells the story better of how to take the leap successfully. Fred's common-sense wisdom and experience shines through this journey of transformation — an excellent read for young and old, and everyone in between."

— Tiff Macklem, dean of the Rotman School of Management, former senior deputy governor of the Bank of Canada

"The lessons you remember are the ones from good storytellers and Fred Dawkins is one of the best. I found myself nodding my head in agreement and smiling as I read *Ageless Entrepreneur*. There is much diversity in entrepreneurs and the lessons on age are equally applicable to the diverse community in understanding our strengths. Underlying the entrepreneurial spirit are self-belief and action."

— David Tsubouchi, former Ontario Minister of Consumer and Commercial Relations, CEO of the Ontario College of Trades, chair of management board, and author of *Gambatte*

"*Ageless Entrepreneur* is a must-read, not only for entrepreneurs, but for anyone who is reinventing their lives. Fred weaves a wonderful true tale demonstrating how age makes little difference in our personal journey. The true journey is our willingness to take risks and grow into the people we are meant to become. Entrepreneurship just so happens to be a great path for many of us."

— Michelle Glover, founder of DreamLife Properties, *The Tea Tree Oil Review*, *Business Women Experts*, and www.girlentrepreneur.com

"Recently I was in the process of selling my historically significant commercial building. During the negotiations with realtors and prospective buyers, poring over lists, namely needs, wants, and conditions, I was overwhelmed and sought a diversion in Fred Dawkins's book. I quickly became immersed in the text. His counsel on the key elements in negotiations awakened in me an appreciation for what was most important for me as well as for the buyer, and the need for flexibility to reach an agreement. I accepted that it truly was a process that had to evolve, and because of his advice I felt empowered and confident to negotiate the sale."

— Elaine Tucker, independent business owner

"One of the biggest trends out there is the retirement of the baby boomers, coupled with rising life expectancy. Fred Dawkins's *Ageless Entrepreneur* takes a *Wealthy Barber*-type storyline approach to describing the 'encore' acts of baby boomers who have left the corporate womb but aren't quite ready (either financially or emotionally) for full-time golf and daytime television. In fact, the story eerily parallels the launch of my own 'encore' entrepreneurial endeavour."

— Jonathan Chevreau, founder of the Financial Independence Hub, formerly editor-in-chief at *MoneySense Magazine*

"In *Ageless Entrepreneur*, author Fred Dawkins maintains that the modern economy, while challenging, is one where opportunities abound. He maintains that seeking out and capitalizing on these opportunities for innovation, entrepreneurship, and intrapreneurship in furtherance of creating and managing your own career is the most important skill any person, whether new to the workforce or entering a new career phase, can seek to attain. This book provides a simple but powerful story to reveal the essential need for interdisciplinary collaboration and mentorship, purposeful career and education choices, and a mindfully entrepreneurial sense of self-awareness in order to succeed. In an elegantly simple approach, Dawkins characters transform themselves, individually and as a group, from an uncertain and unfocused collection of individuals into a dynamic opportunity-identifying alliance. Entrepreneurship is a mindset that can occur at any age and anyone unsure about setting out on their own path should read this book first to be assured that they are in very good company at all times."

— Chris Delaney, business and family wealth strategist, author, and speaker

"Is it a crisis or an opportunity? The economy taking shape is not one that is creating enough jobs for those at the extreme edges of the labour market. The young are trying to claw their way into careers that do not involve serving coffee, all the while wondering what it is that they should really want to do. At the more senior end of the market, many are either being forced to figure out new careers, or worrying that they will have to soon. Entrepreneurship could offer a solution to both groups, but only if they have the nerve and the skills to pursue it. In *Ageless Entrepreneur*, Fred Dawkins offers practical advice and help to both groups in the form of an engaging and entertaining read."

— Linda Nazareth, economist and author of *Economorphics*, formerly senior economic analyst, BNN

"*Ageless Entrepreneur* is a must-read for anyone wanting to bring themselves up to speed with the challenges facing today's workforce. Fred has identified precisely the issues facing millennials, boomers, and those affected in between by the change in economy over the last several years. The way he has put a story to the issues that need to be addressed makes the book a very enjoyable read. We are not in the industrial age any longer, but we have an educational system and a societal belief that the only way to work is to work for an employer. Fred brings to light how our thinking has to change from being a victim, and to not just survive, but to take control of the future by embracing entrepreneurial thinking in order to thrive in the twenty-first century."

— Debbie Ruston, owner of *The Success Educator*

"We live in a time of significant economic transition; we all experience it but two age groups feel it more than others, the pre twenty-five and the post fifty-five. The young can't get their careers started and the older find their careers ending before they are ready. In *Ageless Entrepreneur*, Fred Dawkins tells the engaging story of what happens when members of these two groups are brought together. The results will surprise, inform, and, best of all, inspire you."

— Mark Zimmerman, senior advisor and CIO, MaRS Discovery District

THE ENTREPRENEURIAL EDGE

AGELESS
Entrepreneur

NEVER TOO EARLY, NEVER TOO LATE

Fred Dawkins

DUNDURN
TORONTO

Editor: Jennifer McKnight
Design: Courtney Horner
Cover Design: Laura Boyle
Cover Image: © alexskopje/ iStockphoto.com
Printer: Webcom

Library and Archives Canada Cataloguing in Publication

Dawkins, Fred, 1945-, author
    Ageless entrepreneur : never too early, never too late / Fred Dawkins.

(The entrepreneurial edge ; 3)
Issued in print and electronic formats.
ISBN 978-1-4597-2824-0

    1. Entrepreneurship. 2. Success in business. 3. Career development.
I. Title. II. Series: Entrepreneurial edge (Series) ; 3

HB615.D39 2015   658.4'21   C2015-900580-9
                                                C2015-900581-7

1 2 3 4 5   19 18 17 16 15

We acknowledge the support of the **Canada Council for the Arts** and the **Ontario Arts Council** for our publishing program. We also acknowledge the financial support of the **Government of Canada** through the **Canada Book Fund** and **Livres Canada Books**, and the **Government of Ontario** through the **Ontario Book Publishing Tax Credit** and the **Ontario Media Development Corporation**.

VISIT US AT
Dundurn.com | *@dundurnpress* | *Facebook.com/dundurnpress* | *Pinterest.com/dundurnpress*

Dundurn
3 Church Street, Suite 500
Toronto, Ontario, Canada
M5E 1M2

CONTENTS

PREFACE

In business folklore there's an often told tale that sales managers have shared with new recruits for the last three generations. It seems that back in the 1920s, when business was booming, the owner of a large and successful shoe company wanted to expand his business outside of North America. After much discussion it was determined that Africa looked interesting because there was no competition operating in that market. Management decided to send their number one salesman, Eddie O'Brien, who was approaching retirement, to assess the potential. After just a few days they received a very terse telegram from Eddie stating "situation hopeless — nobody wears shoes." Needless to say the project was abandoned.

Thirty years later, after the hardships of the Depression and the Great War, the same company was looking at international markets again and Africa was raised as a possibility. No one was keen to go but they had just hired a young business school graduate named George Carmichael who didn't quite fit in. Off he went, and in about a week George sent back an equally succinct telegram: "Situation fantastic — nobody wears shoes." There's several value lessons in this story related to age, enthusiasm, prison thinking, perspective, and perception, but all relate to recognizing opportunity.

Finding opportunity is a huge key to success at all levels, but it's becoming more difficult. Life is not a dress rehearsal, no matter what your beliefs. Whether you embrace the Abrahamic religions and aim for eternal life in heaven, or an Asian religion that seeks a better life next time around, or you just want to make the most of this one, everything points to specific goals that you need to accomplish in this lifetime. Your beliefs may provide your motivation but it is up to you and you alone to find your way.

Life is about self-determination within the value system that you embrace. Every generation has to adapt to a changing environment that forces individuals to reset goals within revised parameters. Governments change. Religions adjust. Regimes rise and fall. Economies move through boom and bust. All the while we're immersed in evolution. The main difference today is the pace. The one constant is rapid change. The Dark Ages hampered progress for a thousand years; today the fundamentals of every aspect of our lives shift more than once within a generation. Welcome to the world of Big Data. We can't possibly know everything.

In this state of near frenzied transformation, the critical characteristics for success, whether economic, social, religious, or political, are resilience and adaptability. These are the traits of an entrepreneur. We cannot think like Eddie O'Brien. Rigidity and blind faith in the status quo are limitations. This mindset is not limited to business. We are seeing increasing social entrepreneurship for a reason. Entrepreneurial ideas apply to every element of your life and will allow you to dictate your defining moments. Entrepreneurial thinking is at a premium. The rebels of the past have entered the mainstream of the present and will define the future.

Entrepreneurs offer a critical resource that finds ways to succeed under any circumstance, whether within democracy, under a dictatorship, in a feudal society, within communism, and even within religion. Free enterprise is but one system within which entrepreneurs flourish. The mindset of all entrepreneurs is to make things happen, focusing on a combination of opportunity and determination. We do not always know the way but we are committed to find a way, solving all types of problems in the process. George Carmichael saw opportunity because he needed to prove himself. Eddie O'Brien had nothing to prove.

Society has much to say about entrepreneurial opportunities but determination exists within the individual regardless of the context. It is a life philosophy that can be taught. The most important skill you can learn in this dynamic world is the ability to create and manage your career and your life, which means constantly looking for and recognizing opportunity, followed by finding ways to capitalize.

This mantra of mine is particularly true if you are in either of the shoulder groups of the work force; whether at the point of starting your career or facing the prospect of winding your work life down while needing to extend it. Both of these groups are thirsting for opportunity. The youth of today are facing barriers to entry that impede the start of their careers. In contrast the reality for seniors is that freedom 55 is one of those moving targets making it a necessity to extend their careers while downsizing, outsourcing, and technology are forcing them to the sidelines. There is no room for prison thinking in this "New Era of Entrepreneurship," where necessity dictates the need to identify opportunity and each of us must *carpe diem.*

ACKNOWLEDGEMENTS

Writing this series has given me the opportunity to validate my career by sharing a lifetime of experiences as a serial entrepreneur at a time when entrepreneurship has moved into the economic forefront. I am grateful for the opportunity to have observed and interacted with the past two MBA classes at The Rotman School of Management at the University of Toronto in the Creative Destruction Lab program, as well the chance to observe the progress of the ventures that participate in the Lab. Both of these groups inspire confidence as to what can be accomplished in Canada in the near future. With almost 400,000 Canadians living and working in Silicon Valley it's time to focus on retaining our best and most brilliant talent. Too much of our intellectual capital has left looking for opportunity lacking at home. The Lab, under the direction of Professor Ajay Agrawal, is an important initiative in this regard and it's working.

I would like to thank David Axon for sharing his experience with me regarding Juniors for Seniors, the business he started as a summer job. Resilient teens like David give me confidence that entrepreneurship is alive and well in the next generation, as it needs to be.

I am also grateful for the opportunity to interact with the developing entrepreneurship program at the University of Guelph and would like to thank Maryam Latifpoor-Keparoutis, the development manager of the engineering faculty, for her support and for introducing me to a wealth of excellent contacts at the university. As much as the recognition from the academic community means to me, these books are written for the average person engaged in the traditional economy. They are intended to prepare anyone from a high school dropout to a Ph.D. for the demands and requirements of living the life of an entrepreneur — an ambitious goal. The narrative style has been well received but only the reader can make a final determination of the result.

Whatever that opinion may be the most important acknowledgement I can make is to my wife, Karin, and all of my family for their ongoing and unconditional support of my career in general and for the books in this series in particular. This book, like every one I have written or will write, is dedicated to Karin.

INTRODUCTION

Our perception of aging is determined largely by the society in which we live. In most Asian cultures old age is celebrated. Once you have reached sixty, it's incumbent in some countries for your oldest son to be responsible for you. In my travels to India I can remember having conversations about this with a number of friends who were looking forward to the possibility. In areas like these the elderly are revered for their sage wisdom and their advice is sought after. Isn't this what all of us want in our old age; respect with no responsibility? In the west we seem to be all too willing to look at the elderly as a used up resource, out of date, to be discarded, a potential burden as opposed to a source of wisdom. Now to compound things the old and the young are being forced to compete for jobs, at least indirectly. By staying in the work force seniors are hampering the start of many young careers in a limited job market. Inadequate resources for retirement and increasing life expectancy give them little choice. The two groups are now rivals ... or are they?

From the time we run our first lemonade stand or take on a paper route to the point where we are finally able to join the host of retired volunteers serving our community, we flirt with a path of self-determination and independence, seeking out problems to solve. Most of us take great satisfaction in solving even the smallest problem. It's tempting to conclude that this is an inherent element of the human spirit. In that sense we are all entrepreneurial, fostering a desire to break down barriers and make things happen. This trait is never more evident than when our children or our grandchildren are facing any type of problem. Nothing can stop us from helping them. The contradiction is that many of us don't pursue the solutions to our own issues with the same level of commitment. We let fear creep into decisions and prevent us from acting in our own interests, yet we have a mindset that's totally instinctive, prompting us to protect our offspring from any threat. Somehow we find ways to defeat that danger; we will find a way at virtually any cost. In the west the old are responsible for the young. Being a parent and grandparent is a life sentence. One we willingly assume. Where our children are concerned there is no prison thinking. The essence of being entrepreneurial is this very mindset that does not allow us to fail, not some inherent skill set. Embracing this philosophy of accomplishment will impact the way you approach life — find the way!

For the past century the west has fostered the belief that our free enterprise society, tempered by education, will ensure unlimited opportunity for our youth. Western society has also created the expectation that one's senior years will be spent enjoying a golden age of leisure in retirement. We have dreamt up a near utopia — easy entry to great opportunities for the young and a graceful exit into a full life of travel and relaxation at the end of the line. One problem: no generation has achieved this idyllic vision — not one. Oh, it looked like the boomers would set the standard but even their aspirations faltered in 2008 with the fall of investment values and the loss of confidence that followed. Both of these premises, the stuff of idealistic dreams, are currently under attack.

Ageless Entrepreneur tells the story of two distinct groups of characters struggling with the new realities of our economy. The younger group of four reflects the cynicism and frustration inherent in the high rate of youth unemployment in the western economies as they struggle to launch their careers. The older group of five mirrors the increasing need for seniors to extend their careers because of inadequate savings/pensions in the face of greater life expectancy. Inability to retire is in danger of becoming an unpleasant certainty. If only the older group could step aside the opportunities for the younger one would begin to improve. Obviously the issues for these two factions are different but they're also conjoined. Or are they? In *Ageless Entrepreneur* the two cohorts merge to attack their problems under the mentorship of Sam Macleod, a serial entrepreneur and mentor who has recently launched a new career of his own as an author.

The issues and challenges that are pressing for all the characters are reflected through the perspective of the narrator, one of the five seniors, Nick Valeriote, who is instrumental in bringing Sam back to his hometown to speak about his book on entrepreneurship. Many lessons are learned that are relevant to anyone who is aspiring to become an entrepreneur, regardless of age, whether through opportunity or out of necessity. The most important skill we can learn today is the ability to create and manage our own career. It is never too early to start or too late to achieve.

CHAPTER ONE

Return of an Icon

June 22, 2014

The last time I had seen Sam Macleod was almost thirty years ago at my brother's funeral. Before that my most vibrant memory of him was from twenty years earlier on the day he left town and went to university. As a boy I worshipped Sam. He and my brother Gary were inseparable and at seven years younger I followed the two of them around like a puppy dog waiting to lick up their scraps, loving every minute of it. Most of the time they treated me well. Occasionally they would lose patience. Once when they were training for football they decided to take turns making me run downhill while they tossed the ball as far over my head as they could, making me chase it all over the empty parking lot they liked to use to practice.

Every time I faithfully brought the ball back and then ran as hard as I could to catch up to their passes always thinking that I was just too slow. I had no idea why they were killing themselves laughing. Every scraped knee made them howl more. Only later when I was playing on the same high school team that they had left behind, having a few young admirers of my own, did I realize that the scrapes and scratches from chasing down the ball were a by-product of their solution for keeping me out of the way for a while. I never resented it. Years later, when I finally clued in, the memory of the whole scene made me laugh. I still smile when I think about it. However, when we played neighbourhood pickup, no matter what the sport, Sam always took me for his team, even when no one else wanted the little kid to play. The two friends guided me through my early life protecting me in the process, all the while making me feel special.

Then my balloon burst. I was crushed to find out that Sam was leaving town because his father had been promoted and the family was moving to Toronto. His friendship with my brother continued as they drifted in and out of each other's lives. Both of them became intercollegiate wrestlers in the same weight class. Sam won two titles, Gary one. Sam went to the prominent University of Toronto while Gary was in one of the first graduating classes at Brock University. Competition provided a source of good-natured ribbing between them, often with an edge. At the time their never-ending banter focused on the merit of the universities they attended, in Sam's case mirroring the presumption of superiority of the establishment, confronted by Gary featuring the audacity of the new kid on the block. Neither would give ground so neither could ever win. As for the wrestling, they were each other's major supporter until they met on the mat.

After graduation the lifelong buddies went in very different directions. Gary took a job with a large national bank. At first Sam floundered, teaching school for a year before going back to get an MBA. In the midst of his grad school exams his father-in-law died. Within weeks Sam joined his brother-in-law in the small family business.

Gary really gave him static about the decision, arguing that Sam was making a huge mistake. The big city banker thought his friend had too much talent to squander on a small independent business. Sam couldn't explain his interest beyond saying he "just had to try." He never looked back and thrived in the partnership, awash in independence. Sam and his brother-in-law turned that first business into a flourishing manufacturing plant that employed several hundred.

From that point on, my two mentors saw each other less frequently as their lives evolved in different directions. When they did see each other they engaged in a different ongoing debate focused on the merits of large multinational businesses versus those of small flexible companies that create jobs. From Sam's perspective the banks owed the small business community more support. From Gary's point of view small companies were vulnerable, involving high risk and lower return as the banks increasingly moved into more profitable areas of the economy. This became the second issue they would never agree on.

We all have those moments when we realize that through incredible neglect years have gone by and we have been so wrapped up in our day-to-day existence that we've been ignoring some of the most important people in our lives. How does that happen? Whatever the reason, Sam and Gary were no different, so out of guilt they continued to reconnect from time to time, with the gaps in between growing longer. When they did see each other, both quickly found the comfort zone inherent in a life-long friendship and they enjoyed short bursts of renewal, always highlighted by good-natured ribbing, neither of them giving nor asking for any reprieve. As for me, my ties with Sam were pretty well cut except for the odd time I ran into him by accident on one of his visits to see Gary.

And then my brother died. Just like that, Gary was gone at forty — no warning, no chance to say goodbye, just gone. The word "shock" barely scratches the surface of the feelings of trauma and disbelief.

At the funeral neither one of us could carry on a conversation. One inexplicable, destructive coronary thrombosis and we were sharing the loss of a best friend. Describing Gary's death as premature hardly begins to explain our mutual feelings of anger followed by despair. For me, I had lost an older brother who nurtured me like a third parent, one who always understood me. For Sam it was the loss of his oldest and closest friend. We all have one — that special pal, one of many with whom you shared your childhood but somehow this was the one friendship that survived. The loss was an unspoken common bond between Sam and I, and it had remained just that until this moment. Those feelings of abject despondency were the last thing I had shared with Sam.

Today my old idol was coming home.

CHAPTER TWO

The Renewal of a Lifetime Allegiance

His return was my idea.

In his retirement Sam had reinvented himself yet again. Gary's friend had lived the life of a serial entrepreneur grounded in self-determination. From the age of twenty-three he had been involved in a series of successful small businesses, more or less under the radar, but I had kept track. However, it was my nephew Mark, Gary's son, who showed me a YouTube video of his uncle Sam giving a webinar on entrepreneurship focused on reaching, of all people, the millennial generation, kids like my grandchildren. How unlikely was that, for any old boy to be trying? Not to mention Sam. Next I discovered that he had published a book intended to encourage more people to consider entrepreneurship, offering shared experiences to better prepare those who tried. I decided that it was time for him to come home and share his story with the people who knew him first.

I had stayed put after attending the University of Guelph, taking a job with a local family-owned manufacturing firm, moving up to a senior management role in an organization that became my lifelong employer, all with the expectation of acquiring equity. I thought I was the owner's succession plan. He found something better. Five years ago my revered boss, the architect of our long-term, two-way trust relationship announced the acquisition of *our* company by an American firm. Two years later the parent made an announcement of their own confirming *our* closure as they elected to consolidate operations. Their final act of kindness was the proverbial golden handshake. Equity was not to be mine. I dawdled around for the next two years doing some token consulting for them during the windup before electing to use my termination bonus as a down payment and buy a vacant 40,000 square foot industrial building, determined to control my own destiny.

It took me a lifetime to realize why Sam "just had to try" that little business when his father-in-law died. Self-determination, based on action, beats waiting for a promotion that might never come, hands down. I finally got the idea the hard way. Having control, even when burdened by total responsibility, beats the game of playing politics in an organization controlled by others. My experience offered quite a contrast from the diversity of Sam's career, but ultimately I had seen the light. It was probably too late for me to achieve much, but better late than never.

My interest in his book went well beyond our old friendship. Sam was mentoring me again after all these years. He just didn't know it. His target was a younger audience but there was unspent energy in many people my age along with a thirst for achievement, and in some cases an economic need to support a forced retirement.

I was to pick him up at the train station. Then we would head off to his presentation sponsored by the local chamber of commerce. Sam was speaking on "The New Era of Entrepreneurship," one of his favourite topics. Afterward he would be signing books and mixing with old and new friends alike. About a hundred and fifty people were expected.

I had orchestrated the event with total confidence but now I was nervous. How well did Sam remember me? Was he just coming to sell books? What should I say to him? It had been so long. My emotions were raw as a siege of memories attacked my thoughts.

It started to rain, which somehow seemed appropriate, and then he was there walking down the platform toward me. It was reassuring to see the wide smile on the face of a man who still had the power to make me shake in the knees with the fear of disappointing him. Old habits die hard. Naturally, he spoke first.

"Well, Nick, I never would have thought that the kid Gary and I took out on Halloween fifty years ago and pushed over outhouses with would turn out to be such a respectable-looking dude."

And with that offhand remark the ice was broken. There was a smile on my face matching the one on his as we shook hands and embraced with real feeling as only old friends could do.

"I'd almost forgotten that night. Gary made me promise never to tell a soul because if Mom and Dad found out he was in big trouble and I would be in worse. The two of you terrorized me that night. I was maybe seven and I was sure I was going to fall into one of those shithouses after you pushed it over, or worse, get caught by the owners."

Sam was laughing out loud.

"Gary was furious that we had to take you but we made sure you didn't cramp our style. We even collected some candy for you to keep you quiet.… I still miss him."

There was an awkward silence, maybe the only one that happened over the next few weeks. Then I changed the subject.

"So welcome back, Sam. Are you all ready to give the big performance for the home crowd?"

That seemed to relax him.

"Actually I am. Some people can't wait to grab a platform and speak to an audience. That's definitely not me. Give me one-on-one or a small group anytime. I hated these bigger crowds at first. Too many people are easily impressed that you wrote a book regardless of what it's about. I don't like the attention, but I'm finally getting used to it. We should have a friendly audience today, don't you think?"

We had fallen easily into a comfortable pattern of familiar conversation. While your body ages your mind refuses to recognize it. When you reconnect with someone like Sam, no matter how long it's been, your mind jumps right back to where it once was. As we drove to the Legion building, where a welcoming crowd of admirers was waiting, we talked mainly about the problem at hand: his upcoming speech. But along the way Sam worked in enough penetrating questions to find out what I had done in my career and what my goals were now. He had a way of drawing people out with ease. It was painless.

Before I knew it we'd arrived, but not before having agreed to an early dinner together before Sam caught a later train back to the city. Then I handed him over to the emcee for the day, Jim Hammond, and moved to the back of the room to take in the whole event and watch my old friend perform. I had declined to introduce him. My goal was to observe, not to get wrapped up in participating. Besides, I had an idea for Sam that I wanted to bring up over supper. Part of it depended on what he had to say that day.

CHAPTER THREE

No Disappointment

For a moment I regretted my decision to let someone else introduce my brother's best friend. Jim's introduction was factual but lacked any personal connection. Gary would not have been pleased with me. No one else seemed to notice, so as Sam took the podium he received loud and warm response, one reserved for a local boy who has made good. His opening remarks suggested he was relaxed, seemingly reassured by the welcoming crowd in front of him. Quite a change from the shy kid who grew up a few blocks away. The scene reminded me of one of Gary's favourite jibes delivered often to Sam to gain back an advantage. As a teenager Sam was a jock but despite his popularity, for his first date, he had to convince Gary to phone and ask the girl to go out with him. He couldn't do it himself, just another thing my brother had held over his head for years. Today he was a different man, comfortable in his own skin. On the drive over he told me that he'd developed a PowerPoint presentation with visuals that people seemed to like.

"I really prefer a conversational interview situation but I've developed my own style for public speaking; basically I speak to the slide. That way I forget about the audience and stay focused."

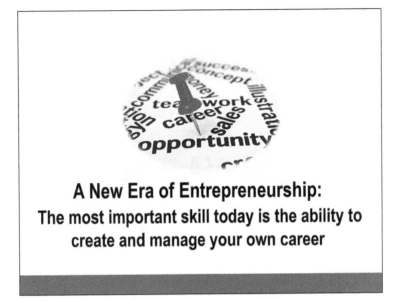

A New Era of Entrepreneurship:
The most important skill today is the ability to create and manage your own career

As the first slide appeared on the screen, I knew he was nervous but he hid it well. The image was a picture of Sam from a focus group he conducted at the University of Toronto. The writing beside the photo was a quote from his book: "The most important skill today is the ability to create and manage your own career." That was one of his dominant themes and one that he hammered home at every opportunity. As the crowd quieted down Sam began.

"It's one of life's little ironies that writers write because they don't like to speak. However, once you get a book published you soon get engaged in a process called 'shameless self-promotion' and before you know it you find yourself talking to anyone who will listen, whenever and wherever they want, including a bunch of old friends in your hometown."

At that point there were a few chuckles and the stage had been set.

"When I was approaching retirement a few years ago, the only two things on my bucket list were to write a book then to get it published. As it turns out, those are two very different things. The most important advice I received was to write about something you know. For me that meant writing about my career and the experiences that I had along the way. My first reaction was 'Who would be interested in *my* career?' It's been anything but high profile. In the meantime I started doing some pro bono consulting in my own way. I am grateful for the opportunities that I've had in my own businesses and I wanted to encourage others. My idea was to explain the world of small business to people considering it, so I started a series of short programs — no charge — for anyone who was interested, but limited to three at a time. That's when I met Tim Davidson; he was in one of those first informal sessions. Before I knew it he had me doing online seminars or webinars. Some of you may have seen one of them.

"It turns out my career is relevant. You can see some of the highlights: forty-five years as an entrepreneur in several businesses in different industries. One of those was in the first wave that faced serious off-shore competition. We had to make a tough choice: either sell, if we could, or move the company offshore and manufacture overseas. Fortunately we were able to sell. Within ten years the domestic industry was decimated. I had to reinvent myself several times over the years but that's the new normal we all face today. Now my goal is to encourage the broadest possible use of entrepreneurial thinking because we are already in this new era of entrepreneurship we're discussing today. That goes well beyond starting or running a business. I can't stress enough how important it is for every individual to become their own brand, making good strategic decisions along the way. So entrepreneurship for all, but entrepreneur's such an awkward word isn't it?"

Once again several people nodded as Sam took the opportunity to drink some water. As he continued another slide popped up: "Understanding Entrepreneurship."

"It's a long word, sixteen letters. If you hashtag it that makes

Understanding Entrepreneurship

seventeen characters, which plays havoc with your Tweets. Oh yes, I'm on Twitter. Every author has to be."

There were many smiles and a few chuckles around the room as many in the audience, including myself, conjured up images of retirement age Sam pounding out tweets on his laptop.

"When you write about entrepreneurs, as I have, you are constantly using the words 'entrepreneur,' 'entrepreneurial,' or 'entrepreneurship' because there just aren't good alternatives. If you look up most words in the thesaurus there will be eight or ten close options and you can choose the one that works the best for your situation. But there's not even one appropriate entry for entrepreneurship — there are *no* good single word alternatives. One of the few alternatives given is 'free enterprise,' and that's just plain wrong. Free enterprise does not define the word, it's just one environment in which entrepreneurs thrive, but I assure you they will do well in any environment from dictatorship to communism because they're problem solvers. In fact, in offering up that equivalent the thesaurus is reinforcing the idea that entrepreneurship only applies to business,

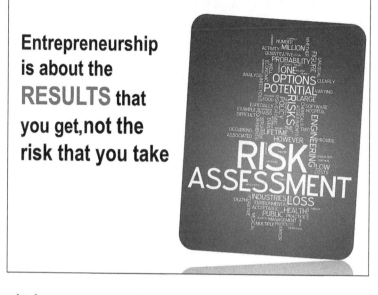

which is just wrong. The guiding principles of entrepreneurship can be applied to every aspect of life. Take control and make things happen.

"Finally, if you look up the word's derivation you will find that the word 'entrepreneur' derives from the French verb *entreprendre* which means 'to undertake.' However, if I was encouraging all of you to become undertakers very few of you would have come today, local boy or not."

Most of the audience laughed at that.

"More than just awkward, the word is intimidating and it has an element of mystique about it. With all of these complications, it's no wonder that the concept is so misunderstood. Worst, all of the publicity about entrepreneurs revolves around specific types that get all the attention. Most of the time we hear about the gamblers and misfits who strike out on their own either because they can't or don't want to conform. Or we read about the tech entrepreneurs tied to the world of venture capital where only one in ten succeeds. Together these two kinds have helped create the stereotypical idea that entrepreneurs have to take huge risks and suffer a high rate of failure. We rarely hear about the many other types of entrepreneurs running businesses in so many other areas in the mainstream economy. We only hear about them when we need them, at times when unemployment is high and we need them for job creation. Successful entrepreneurs in the traditional economy manage their risk and avoid failure. Being an entrepreneur is about the results that you get, not the risk that you take."

There was some polite applause at that comment. Most people, myself included, were dissuaded from independent business because of the perceived risk. I could remember Sam and Gary arguing about this perception years ago. Sam continued on.

"Risk should not be a barrier to entry for anyone, whether in business, in social entrepreneurship, or in life itself. Emphasizing the need for risk makes for bad decisions, encouraging some people to take ridiculous risks because they think they have to, while other people let meaningful opportunities die because they're risk averse. There is always an inverse relationship between risk and reward. That's why only one in ten venture capital investments succeed so well, or, in other words, just 10 percent of the time do we see success in the risky high-tech community. High risk can provide high rewards if success is the result but the odds are poor. The chances are better elsewhere, but remember, having ideas just makes you a dreamer. Making those ideas a reality is what converts you to an entrepreneur. Every idea is not an opportunity. Every opportunity is not viable. Sustainability is a critical part of assessing any idea. Beyond the risk perception, there are so many myths about entrepreneurs that need to be dismissed because we're in a new age where entrepreneurship has become critical. Why do I say that? Well, consider the world we live in. The two most dominant economic factors are globalization and technology.

"We live in a very competitive world. When I started my career you could run a very successful business entirely within

Globalization & Technology

five hundred miles of your home base. Technology was gaining momentum but it was evolving at a manageable pace. That was fifty years ago. Now there is one constant we can count on in our lives — rapid change. We have to chase markets around the world. We have to compete with competitors who we don't know or understand. Technology is moving at warp speed as we flirt with a quantum world. Welcome to the era of Big Data. It's no longer possible to know everything. In fact, most of us don't understand much of what we do know. Success in our fast-paced society requires different traits than in the past. We all must become more adaptable and resilient. These are the traits of entrepreneurs who in a variety of ways follow a different life philosophy than others. Entrepreneurs will not give up until they *find* a way; they don't have to *know* the way. It's about the mindset, not the skill set. Entrepreneurs never ask *if* they will accomplish something but jump right to *how* they will do it. They literally make things happen instead of waiting for them to happen. Every problem is an opportunity, and through determination entrepreneurs are problem solvers. All of us can and must learn to think this way. There is no room for prison thinking in a world dominated by change. The ability to find a way within the quagmire of ever expanding knowledge is becoming an essential skill."

There was a minor disruption around the room as a number of people muttered comments to their neighbour. It appeared that Sam had hit a nerve for many.

"For more than fifty years our business schools have been working on what is emerging as a flawed model that's producing executives for large corporations mired in a culture of control. In my college days the word entrepreneur was never used. Twenty-five years ago it was rarely used. Now every college and university offers programs in entrepreneurship. There is a rush to find effective ways to teach the fundamentals and a pressing need for mentorship from people like me who have lived the life. The rush to embrace entrepreneurs started in earnest after the recession hit in 2008. Downturns call for corrections. When a recession attracts the adjective 'great,' correction needs to be swift and decisive. Our dominant and biggest organizations were failing us. Business leaders were preoccupied with profits and bonuses,

Why is entrepreneurship becoming mainstream?

making them far too removed from the impact of change. Finally, our education system recognizes the need to produce a different graduate who can embrace change, but at this stage our efforts are running behind the rate of societal change. We are engaged in a continuous process of rebirth, meaning we need to educate new-age renaissance men and women — people who can master a wide range of changing circumstances.

"There are lots of implications from our changing world. First let's consider the micro world of the individual. Globalization had brought millions of people into the world work force, increasing the supply of labour. At the same time technology, through robotics, mechanization, and artificial intelligence, has reduced the demand for labour. Together these trends are putting downward pressure on real wage rates. The rewards are accruing to capital at the expense of labour, helping create a small class of super-rich while the middle class is under siege, reverting back to historic norms, which is not good for the majority of us. We have a serious structural unemployment issue in the west for unskilled and semi-skilled labour and no governments are addressing it. Job stability is disappearing. There are barriers for young people trying to get their careers started, while older people are being forced out of the labour force at a time when they need to extend their careers. As survivors of the Depression my parents' generation developed a thirst for stability, which they passed on down the line. We've reached an era where we have to trade in stability for agility. As the first fades the other becomes essential.

"For all of these reasons each of us has to become our own brand. There is no upside to sitting on the sidelines and following the crowd. Most people will change jobs several times in their career. To do this well and maintain some upward mobility we have to make good strategic decisions: take those jobs for the right reasons, develop the skills to create and manage your own career. These choices are the essence of being entrepreneurial. If you feel you can't do this, try anyway and make yourself link up with people who can. Big business will not tackle the structural unemployment issue. Multi-nationals invest for profit maximization, but entrepreneurs tend to invest locally and will see opportunity there when people who are structurally unemployed are willing to work for less. We are a key part of the transition to a true global economy and we will create jobs when and where neither big government nor big business can."

Sam was twenty minutes into his presentation but no one in the room appeared restless. His slides were effective. He had told me that pictures constituted more than 50 percent of the impact of a PowerPoint, but his approach of talking to the slides magnified the impact of both his words and the images. I hadn't expected his insight to impact me quite this way.

"So let's look at the *big* picture — the macro world of large organizations and big government. We had a revelation in 2008. We were all scared ... scared enough to support bailing out revered institutions like GM and AIG. For God's sakes, it was not so long before that GM had been the nineteenth biggest economy in the world. Only eighteen countries generated more

economic activity than GM. They were living in an insulated world but those in the ivory towers could not hide. Decisions made to maximize short-term profits came back to haunt them. So they invented a convenient new term. Perhaps 'Too Big to Fail' really just means 'Too Big!' These behemoths we've created work to a ten-year plan in a world that is moving beyond them. Why, I bet you can name a dozen different jobs that didn't exist ten years ago, most of them related to the Internet or senior health. Big companies can't adapt fast enough. Right now they are relying on outsourcing and acquisition for flexibility. Corporate culture has to change. Instead of suppressing individualism managers now need to nurture and encourage it. Mavericks should be welcomed not shunned. There is a pressing need for disruptors, or 'intrapreneurs,' people willing to challenge the status quo, to bring entrepreneurial thinking into both large firms and government. This will not come easily to organizations that rely on systems and rigid structure as agents of control. But it will happen. It will come from the top down, and it will gain momentum from the new graduates coming out of college and university who have embraced the need for and the mindset of entrepreneurship. One can only hope."

At this point there were several hands in the air begging to ask questions, so Jim Hammond interrupted to confirm there would be time for questions when Sam finished before indicating that Sam should continue. Sam was revved, seemingly oblivious to the interruption.

"Incidentally, the good news for individuals is that both outsourcing and acquisition create opportunities for entrepreneurs to either provide services or to build an innovative startup and sell it at a major premium. Overall, the net result of our dynamic world is that we now see an expanding spectrum of entrepreneurship. Traditionally, startups stem from opportunities like those I just mentioned, but increasingly we are seeing new and different forms of entrepreneurship arising out of necessity. I salute and support every type of these new entrepreneurs. You don't have to be a superstar to be an entrepreneur. That's just one more misconception we need to get past. The image of entrepreneurs that the public perceives today is much too centred on the tech world.

"There is a difference between innovation and entrepreneurship. They are far from one and the same, which confuses many. Some great innovations never make it to market. The iPad was a great innovation, and it has led to hundreds of thousands of applications designed by individuals to solve problems at many different levels. Some of these apps have turned into meaningful businesses. For every major tech innovation there will always be thousands of entrepreneurs out there solving real problems by applying that technology. The tech world is fast and furious — a constant race to get to market before anyone else, highlighted by terms like 'accelerator,' 'incubator,' and my personal favourite, 'burn rate.' I love that one. It tells potential investors when you will run out of money, not exactly highlighting your strengths, just prior to negotiating a terms sheet. I equate it to doing a

bungee jump without securing the top end while shouting out 'I'm going to hit the ground in thirty seconds,' hoping that someone will be listening and care enough to grab the bungee cord and save you. Tech is not the real world, but it gets most of the attention and it creates venture capital expectations that make it harder for the rest of us to raise capital. I prefer terms like 'bootstrapping' and 'the lean startup,' which are far more applicable in the mainstream economy where living within your means and getting feedback from real customers is essential. Generating revenue maintains independence. Raising capital sustains bad habits, reduces a sense of urgency, and dilutes equity, which is probably worthwhile in a world where the race to market is a critical element. For the rest of us focusing on sales and the market is much more essential for survival and success.

"Going back to entrepreneurs of necessity as opposed to opportunity, there is a lot of pressure on various groups to find their own way. Need is the problem that must be solved. The solution still depends on recognizing whatever opportunity you might have. Young people are finding serious barriers to entering the work force. Older people are being hit with downsizing and pressure to leave the labour force before they can afford to retire. Mothers are finding that the rate of change makes it hard to get back into the mix. Necessity is the mother of invention and problems are the source of opportunity. So now we have 'mompreneurs' starting home businesses grounded in social networking. We have 'solopreneurs' working alone focused on self-determination with no desire to build a company or employ people. Let's face it, for a modest investment with a laptop, mobile phone, and a website, a resourceful individual can provide meaningful services and/or products on a very competitive, low overhead basis while looking very professional in the process. We also have social entrepreneurs applying an entrepreneurial approach to the problems of society. We expect too much from our governments and look to them for solutions that aren't forthcoming. Social entrepreneurs are result oriented problem solvers who are not seeking re-election — quite a different focus. All of these groups are solving problems and making things happen in the process.

"So welcome to this new era of entrepreneurship. Embrace it. Don't let the myths and misconceptions scare you off. Be your own brand because only you can manage your career and life. More than ever the world needs problem solvers who can act as catalysts to make things happen. Thank you very much for coming today."

The applause was spontaneous. I am sure many people came that day not knowing what to expect, but one of their own had delivered a thought-provoking presentation that they could relate to on a personal level. Sam winked over at me, grateful to have crossed the finish line and ready to answer questions. As for me, I was ready to leave and have Sam to myself for a couple of hours.

CHAPTER FOUR

My Request Gets Deferred

Apparently I was the only one in a hurry. It was time for questions and there were more than I expected, some coming from surprising sources. An old acquaintance of mine, going all the way back to our school days together, a woman named Doris Roberts, reached the microphone before anyone else. She was a couple of years younger than I, so almost sixty. Doris was an unlikely candidate for entrepreneur school. She'd worked her entire life as a receptionist, most of that time at a local real estate office. I knew her boss, and from time to time I ran into her around town. Why would she be interested in entrepreneurship?

"Hello, Sam. Doris Roberts, maybe you remember me. Very interesting talk. I've wanted to start something of my own but I've been kind of afraid. I guess I thought you had to have it in you. So are entrepreneurs born into it or can this economic wonder drug of yours really be taught?"

Doris quickly sat down having used up all the courage she could summon.

"I do remember you, Doris, and your older sister Susan."

There were a few chuckles around the room because a few of us remembered Sam dating Susan and Doris tagging along.

"It's an age-old dilemma Doris, but the answer is both born *and* made, like almost any other talent. But the main point is that entrepreneurship can be taught! It needs to be taught and fortunately it is being taught. If you can embrace the mindset and dig deep for determination you'll be on your way. Stop thinking about why you can't do something and find ways to do it. Start in your personal life. Keep looking for real opportunities and you will do it! Most people are so busy living their lives that they don't see opportunity when it's right in their face. Remember, every problem is an opportunity. The solution doesn't have to be earth shattering to be meaningful."

The next question was asked by a young fellow that I didn't recognize. He looked like he was a student.

"Well, sir, thank you for coming today. Do you believe that it's possible to become an entrepreneur right out of school?"

Sam was smiling at the boy, encouraging him through his demeanour, pleased to see his interest.

"The short answer is yes. The broader answer is that it's more difficult when you're right out of school. What's your name and how far have you gone in school?"

The boy was staring at the floor, reluctant to answer.

"Dominic, sir. I just finished high school, but I can't see going to college or university. I have to borrow money to do it. My sister just graduated from Guelph and she can't get a job. I don't want to waste four years piling up debt for nothing like she has."

Sam looked concerned.

"Well you're not alone. Youth unemployment is a critical issue right now. This is the exact point where managing your career starts. If you research trends in the work force you'll find areas where we need more talent. Then if you choose your courses carefully you'll have a better chance of getting a job after college or university. That's why it's an advantage to think like an entrepreneur and start making strategic decisions early. Never start a business that can't be viable. Never take courses that don't provide a path to a future. That's common sense that most ignore. Education is never a waste. With it your opportunities increase. Getting it develops determination. It takes commitment to graduate.

"But, if you don't feel you should commit to school or just can't afford it, here are a couple of ideas for you. Consider apprenticing for a skilled trade. You will probably still have to go to school, but if you get started with a tradesman, even in an unskilled role, you might get some financial help from your employer. That will depend on your determination and attitude. Once you have the skill it can often lead to your own business, and the trades are pretty much China proof because these jobs have to be done here.

"Another option is select the jobs you apply for carefully. Work on that entrepreneurial mindset and look for young growing companies that need flexible, resilient people. In other words, find a job where you can hang out and learn from entrepreneurs that are already in the game. If you can develop that positive attitude, these companies will see you as more employable. All of this is about making strategic decisions from the day you start preparing to enter the work force. For you that's today.

"One last point: if anyone is serious about going the entrepreneurial route, no matter what age, they have to do a pretty frank assessment of their personal strengths and weaknesses. Lack of experience is a limitation. But every problem, including being young, is an opportunity. Enthusiasm can carry you far in an open learning environment. Avoid prison thinking. That's something I say often. Those that prejudge limit themselves gratuitously. We face enough barriers without creating more. Young people can get work. Find your strengths, whatever they are, and build on them. Remember the term 'SWOT Analysis.' Constantly reassess the strengths, weaknesses, opportunities, and threats that exist in your business and your personal life. They're dynamic and like the world we live in they'll constantly be changing."

Dominic sat down smiling, encouraged for the moment.

The next question came from another surprising source. Martin Goetz was the managing director of a large local company, which was, like my old employer, a subsidiary of an American firm. He had the reputation for being a demanding, hardnosed manager, very old school. He wasn't really a local but had been transferred into the area by the company almost twenty years ago.

"My name is Martin Goetz. I enjoyed your talk but I'm not sure I agree with you on much of it. Do you really believe that large organizations will embrace entrepreneurship from within?"

Sam had no idea who was asking or what his background was, but he had a strong opinion.

"Well, Martin, there is an old expression I mentioned earlier about necessity being the mother of invention. I like to expand on that by saying if necessity is the mother of invention then opportunity is the father of entrepreneurship. I believe we will see more intrapreneurs and disruptors in large companies because they're already needed. We're approaching a tipping point after which the management culture will be forced to change. Need will create the adjustment. That's the opportunity. Necessity and opportunity will dictate less rigidity and greater adaptability within every organization — large and small. Of course it won't happen quickly because many current managers will resist."

Sam had a pretty good read on Martin, who sat down shaking his head in disbelief. The implication was that he was one of those current managers resistant to change. At least that's what I thought. Not many people in the room were sympathetic. No doubt some felt Sam was idealistic and maybe a little overzealous, but no one really liked Martin. Sam didn't leave it quite there.

"Don't assume that I think everyone can be a full-scale entrepreneur. That would be a pipe dream. Besides, I know that large organizations can never become as flexible or as proactive as small independent businesses. However, business methods inevitably reflect the times. That will mean welcoming more entrepreneurs into the big stage environment and taking a major step toward entrepreneurial thinking across the breadth of these organizations. Business is a war game, very competitive with high stakes. Competition plus a growing source of entrepreneurial graduates will make this change in culture happen. You can ride the crest of the wave or get smashed on the beach resisting it. Frankly, once companies recognize this need they will expand the horizons for those 'in between' people who have ideas and initiative but suppress them to conform because they can't or won't make the leap of faith into an independent business. As Doris suggested, entrepreneurship is being viewed by many as an economic wonder drug for the twenty-first century, and it may well be just that. If we can shift the average masses of talent in the middle away from craving stability and toward embracing the reality of dynamic change, who knows what will be possible. Remember, we need to trade in stability for agility."

Martin was still shaking his head while muttering something under his breath but the rest of the room was quiet, even subdued, reflecting on what they had heard.

There were a ton of questions after that. An old colleague of mine, Paul Groves, asked one that had been plaguing me.

"At what age are you too old to start?"

That proved to be my personal favourite and the short answer augured well for my talk with Sam later.

"It's never too late! If I can become a published author at my age anything is possible."

The next question related to one of Sam's favourite doubts, one that dissuaded many potential entrepreneurs. I didn't recognize the guy who asked it.

"Based on the books I've read a lot of people think you're limiting your upside if you never fail because you haven't taken enough risk. That terrifies me. I can't stand the thought or the humiliation of failing. Is failure really an essential part of succeeding as an entrepreneur?"

I knew this was a sore point with Sam. I had seen his reaction to the same question during one of his webinars.

"Fear of failure's a great motivator. Let's face it, no one likes to fail. But the idea that you have to fail to succeed is more than rationalization, it's a crock. Worse than that, it's one of the myths about being an entrepreneur that scares people like you off. Risk is part of the process, but you have to manage it. Much of the downside is within your control through the decisions that you make. If you make reckless choices failure is more likely. My best advice is to avoid failure if you can and learn from it if you must. We all learn more from failure. That's human nature. When we succeed good results mask our faults and bad habits become ingrained in our methods. When we fail we know we have to change so we analyze what happened, looking for reasons. On the other hand, when we succeed we develop a sense of infallibility. Believe me, 'entrepreneurial infallibility' is a real phenomenon, one that's taken some successful people down the second time around."

Still the questions kept on coming plus there was going to be a book signing. I was concerned there'd be no time to talk to Sam before he left. A twenty-something girl brought up an issue that should have been significant for everyone.

"You mentioned decline in upward mobility. What did you mean by the historical norm for the middle class?"

Sam grimaced before answering that one. How to be frank but not practice fear mongering?

"The thriving middle class as we know it pretty much parallels my life, which means the last seventy years. Before that, capital got the rewards and the rest of us subsisted, trapped in our lower-class lifestyle. There were always exceptions, but they were few. Between technology and education the last seventy years have opened up opportunity for the great unwashed. Thanks to technology the quality of life changed dramatically after the Second World War, and that's continued. Thanks to education, upward mobility for large numbers became a reality, swelling the ranks of the middle class. As opportunity increased entrepreneurs found ways to capitalize. However, with the demand for labour in decline and the supply of labour on the rise, labour as a resource has lost its leverage and capital is already reasserting itself to claim the higher rewards that traditionally accrue to investors. Entrepreneurship depends on opportunity. Determination on its own is not enough unless you're one of exceptionally few. Returning to the historical norm means a decline in opportunity, more barriers to upward mobility, and much greater discrepancy in wealth between the super rich and the rest of us. It's already happening, and fast. Just ask Dominic."

The next question came from the mayor, Margaret Castlefield, who had actually been invited to thank Sam but for some reason had become more engaged than anyone expected. Sam did not know her before, but they'd been introduced when we arrived.

"What is the proper role for government in promoting entrepreneurship?"

Sam laughed at that one.

"Thanks for asking, Madame Mayor. It's a critical concern for both the private and public sectors but the full answer will take much more time than we have today. Without going into the details of how, the challenge for governments at all levels is to work in conjunction with social entrepreneurs to deal with societal issues that create barriers to opportunity. The answer does not lie in making value judgements and investing public funds in a whole range of misguided incentives to get individuals to do what governments want. That removes the test of viability. So first governments need to remove barriers and then get out of the way. The second area where governments can make a contribution is to help create supporting environments or ecosystems that enable entrepreneurs to build successful businesses. The best example of this is what Silicon Valley has become for the tech sector. No other environment in the world creates as much opportunity for the tech industry as the Valley. The experience provides a model for what needs to be done in a whole basket of industries. I would love to discuss this with you later if you want my opinion."

The mayor nodded her head. She seemed genuinely interested.

The next question came from a middle-aged fellow who I'd seen before but couldn't place.

"Given that globalization is likely here to stay, can small companies capitalize on global opportunities?"

Now I remembered. His name was Morgan Davis. He ran a small furniture company that manufactured wooden furniture primarily for Canadian embassies. He shipped around the world but only to Canadian government locations. Sam was encouraging.

"Of course they can. There are like-minded small companies around the world eager to do business. With social media you can find them and you can also research foreign markets for your products."

Sam didn't have time to expand on his answer before Jim Hammond interrupted.

"Sorry Sam, but we have to start winding things up so you can sign some books. We can take three more questions, but I'll ask everyone to keep the questions brief."

There were at least ten more people lined up at the microphones so a few disappointed individuals sat down. The next question came from one of our secondary school principals, David Mills.

"Doesn't something have to give? Can humans really sustain the degree of change you're describing? Can we keep embracing the 24/7 work ethic that is being demanded by employers? I personally don't think so."

Oh boy, that was going to require a longer answer.

"I can't answer that, sir. You're bringing up a serious social issue. As a race we're in danger of becoming victims of our own success. How do we slow things down? I don't have the answer for that. On an individual basis Big Data may well overwhelm us. The prospect of trying to keep pace is certainly becoming more alarming."

Two questions to go. A pregnant woman in her mid-thirties came to the mic.

"Can solopreneurs survive for any length of time, or are they really just a means for transitioning between the real opportunities?" I was pretty sure that I knew how Sam would answer that one.

"As long as outsourcing is an important option for companies, solopreners will thrive. Too many organizations prefer contracting out to increasing employment, and that's actually a win-win situation. As a solopreneur you can have three or more employers all paying you a higher hourly rate than they would if you worked exclusively for them but none of them paying for all of your time. They each pay less but the sum of the parts leaves you with significantly more."

Finally the last question was about to be asked by another teenager, this time a girl.

"I read recently that the federal government has implemented a fast track visa to bring entrepreneurs into Canada. Is this a good idea? We don't have enough jobs for young people as it is. And since I'm last I'll ask a quick follow-up: what makes your book different? Why should I read it?"

Sam laughed at the follow up but patiently addressed both issues.

"Yes, it's a good idea. Entrepreneurs create jobs. More than a hundred countries have policies designed to keep and attract entrepreneurs. There's a worldwide competition for talent going on. I think that I mentioned how many Canadians live and work in Silicon Valley, it's close to 400,000. That's over 1 percent of our population and a much greater percentage of our intellectual capital. We have to find ways to keep our best and most brilliant here and to bring more talent here from other areas. Given the context of our multicultural society we have advantages that will help us attract others. We have both the need and the means to do it, so we must create policies that match.

"As far as the book goes, it's intentionally an easy read. I wrote it as a narrative. We all love stories. It gave me the chance to offer shared experiences to the readers. Experts still argue that there is no replacement for experience in becoming an entrepreneur, but

I believe we can prepare people by giving them the benefit of our experiences in a meaningful way. Readers seem to identify with the characters and relate to their problems. The story provides incidental and painless learning. I am a student of business but I don't like business texts. I think the approach works but time will tell. The challenge for me was to write about a complex subject that's becoming much more critical in a way that almost anyone can understand. Basically a common sense guide to changing your life by taking charge of it."

Finally we were done. The thanks given by the mayor was glowing but brief. We were almost on our way. Except of course Sam spent the next forty-five minutes patiently signing books while I paced back and forth, anxious to just get out of there and present my idea.

CHAPTER FIVE

My Proposal

By the time we left the Legion hall, Sam only had ninety minutes to go before the last train left for Toronto.

"You're a very appealing speaker, Sam. Everyone wants a piece of you when you're done. I'd planned to take you out to a steakhouse but I guess we don't have time. You just talked yourself out of a steak dinner and a nice glass of wine."

Sam was leaning back in his seat, relaxing after the stress of being the centre of attention for the entire afternoon.

"That's all right Nick; I have something better in mind. I was sort of hoping we could go to Gino's. It's been a few years for me but I would love one of those delicious foot-long hot dogs. I must have been five or six the first time my dad took me for one. One of those childhood memories that seemed like it happened yesterday. It took me close to an hour to eat but I finished it. In the process I managed to get mustard all over my shirt and shorts before we got home. Mom was not pleased. Do you still go there?"

Gino's had been around as long as I could remember, having started some time back in the early fifties. The menu never changed, the mainstay being the twelve-inch hot dogs on toasted buns served with a mixture of chopped onions and tomatoes combined with Gino's homemade relish. Gino was a local legend and hero. When we were kids Gino, who was a humble guy that almost everyone liked, made a fortune selling hot dogs, allowing him to close the place down and go to Florida for the winter every year. What a life! There was no need to advertise. He opened like clockwork on the 21st of March, the first day of spring, and stayed open to Thanksgiving. People are still lined to get in when it reopens every year. I take my grandkids there, making them the fourth generation of customers from our family to love those hot dogs. Gino's has long been a tradition, one of the rites of spring.

Sam and Gary loved the place and used to hang out there talking to Gino. At first they used to ride their bikes there. Then as teenagers it became a regular weekend destination with a car full of friends. My first chance to try one of the legendary hot dogs came when I arrived as a passenger on the back of Gary's bike along with Sam and three of their buddies. I was about six.

"Of course I still go there, but I haven't been this year so I'm up for it if that's what you want."

Gino's had changed since Sam had been there. Gino had retired two years before, having stayed with a business that was deep in his heart well into his eighties. Maybe Gino proved a point that it wasn't too late for guys like me. The business was run by his son Dino now. A few years ago they'd built a large deck off to the side of the concrete block building. Last year they paved the parking lot. When we were growing up everyone ate in the car. A lot of people still did.

Sam and I each ordered exactly what we had on my first visit. A hot dog, an order of onion rings, and a chocolate milkshake. Every bit of the order tasted exactly the same as it did the first time enhanced by some great memories and the twisted sense of being a little boy with no responsibilities for a few minutes. Food is memories. That was the appeal of Gino's. You could taste your youth. Then you could share that taste with the next generation and the next generation after that. As we ate in the car for old time's sake, Sam began to reminisce.

"You probably can't remember the old clapboard building that Gino started with, can you? It was one of those old carny-style booths, almost like a fruit stand with wooden shutters that you propped open but closed and locked up at night. He really made something out of nothing. That sign over the door with the painted hot dog is original. I remember when he built this new building, he was so excited. You know, Gino might have been the first real entrepreneur that I met. He was a neat guy, always had time for the kids … the future of the business, he liked to say. Gary and I spent hours here. One year we helped him make his relish. He paid us in hot dogs, fries, and shakes. And look at us; he was right. We were those kids and we're still coming back after all these years. I wish Gary was with us."

I was nostalgic about the place as well and I had my own fond memories of Gino. Most of what I remembered revolved around going there with my dad and Gary, boys' nights out when Mom was off at some ladies club meeting, that kind of stuff. For some reason I was a little afraid of Gino. Later on as an adult it was my 'go to' lunch place on a tough day — an oasis. For some reason I asked Sam an obvious question that used to bug me as a teenager.

"I always wondered why he chose hot dogs. Why wouldn't he have picked pizza or some other Italian food?"

Sam was preoccupied, slurping out the dregs of his milkshake, another reversion to childhood that we would have criticized our own kids or grandkids for doing.

"I understand it completely. Gino wanted to be accepted. His opportunity came by doing something that was already established differently and better. He didn't want to introduce something new, especially right after the war when anything from Europe was suspicious. There's still a lot to be said for that. Entrepreneurs often succeed by finding a different angle to do something for which there's a proven demand. Look at Tim Hortons and Starbucks, two completely different approaches to a proven market. Coffee houses have been around for hundreds of years. Yet there you have two modern versions that are hugely successful, appealing to different segments of the same market. That's one more of the entrepreneurial myths, that you have to invent something new. Finding a better way to tap a proven market reduces the risk."

Sam was sure into this entrepreneurship theme. He was charged up and full of it. How was I to know that Gino's was really a museum of local entrepreneurship? I let Sam continue his walk down memory lane a little longer, but I was getting anxious to bring up my idea.

"My brother-in-law got married on March 21. My wife and I were in the wedding party and your brother Gary was a guest. So guess where we ended up after the reception? That's right. A bunch of us came here in our tails and bridesmaids gowns. Gino couldn't believe that in the midst of the wedding we remembered it was his opening day for the season. That was forty-five years ago. I've only been here a couple of times since but it seems like yesterday, same old Gino's."

I couldn't wait any longer.

"Sam, I need your help and I think I've figured out a way for you to give me some that makes sense for both of us. You sort of skirted around the issue all day today. I told you I took my golden handshake and plunked it into a rental building. I need to make that work. I mean, that's going to be my main source of income over and above Canada Pension Plan and Old Age Security. I may have to run some kind of business there myself, partly because I can't rent all the space and partly because I'm carrying debt from refurbishing the building. I'm trying to figure out what to do and I know I'm not alone. You talked about it today, the idea that people are living longer, haven't saved adequately for their retirement, and consequently need to work longer. That's me, Sam, and quite a few others I know."

I can't really say that he looked surprised. He seemed to be more pensive than shocked.

"Nick, you know I'll try to help you. What do you need? What do you have in mind?"

At this point my stomach was queasy. My great idea was starting to seem more like an imposition than an opportunity. On the other hand, what did I have to lose?

"You might think this is ludicrous, but have you given any thought to mentoring seniors?" I didn't give him a chance to answer. I needed to convince him, and fast. Here I was, a senior, making a pitch to someone older than me. I needed him to invest time, not money. "Seriously, you talk a pretty good game that it's never too late and all, but my age group needs help and guidance quickly. If we knew it all we would have done it before this. I guess my idea came from that last webinar series you did on the family entrepreneur and all the factors involved in joining or running a family business. That was good stuff, full of insights. How about doing something similar on the pros and cons of seniors starting a business? How about doing the prototype for your webinar right here over the summer?"

Dead silence. I held my breath for what seemed like minutes, wracking my brain for something else to say that might seal the deal. Finally he spoke.

"We'd better get moving or I'm going to miss my train."

A whole series of four letter words raced through my brain, all directed at me personally — for being inept, for assuming too much, for not making my case, for expecting too much from Sam, for being so vulnerable at my age, and on and on. Now what? Sam didn't say a thing.

In what seemed like an eternity but was more like five minutes, we were at the station. Listening to him talk all day had lifted my confidence. Now I felt smashed on the proverbial beach he had mentioned in his presentation that afternoon. Did he think that I was actually too late, one of the exceptions to his own rule?

I almost didn't get out of the car to see him off, but at the last minute thought better of it. As we shook hands he looked me square in the eyes and said:

"Of course I'll do it. Not sure if we'll use it as a prototype yet, and I do have some time restrictions this summer. I have to think the idea through to make it fit. For the last few minutes I've been thinking how great it's going to be having you buy me lunch at Gino's every day we do this."

I was stupefied. My old friend had just played me like a fish and I took the bait, hook, line, and sinker. Now he was laughing, killing himself laughing, at my expense. Regardless, I was relieved and back to being optimistic.

"Keep your head up Macleod — there'll be plenty of chances for me to get even this summer," I threatened.

CHAPTER SIX

Setting the Framework

In the next few days I learned two distinct things about my old friend Sam. First, he liked to stay up late, which I should have remembered. Second, he preferred to write memos at his convenience and was now a lover of emails sent at any time day or night. Good thing my son had given me a new iPad Mini for Christmas because Sam expected me to answer back right away. The next morning following our exchange at the train station I had four emails when I woke up: one spam and three from Sam. As time went on there were times I wasn't sure what I liked better, spam or Sam. One you delete for sure the other could be tempting. It took over thirty emails to firm up our plans.

Sent Tues 06/23/14 12:41 AM

From: Sam Macleod (sammacsays@gmail.com)
To: Nick Valeriote (nvaleriote1952@sympatico.ca)
Subject: Getting started

Hi Nick,
Thanks for your hospitality today actually yesterday, especially at Gino's. Have a few questions to resolve about your idea. When? Where? Who?
Talk to you soon,
Sam

Sent Tues 06/23/14 1:52 AM

From: Sam Macleod (sammacsays@gmail.com)
To: Nick Valeriote (nvaleriote1952@sympatico.ca)
Subject: More getting started

Hi Nick,
Been thinking some more. A few more questions. How many people? What are your goals? How many sessions are you thinking? Waiting to hear back,
Sam

Sent Tues 06/23/14 6:33 AM

From: Sam Macleod (sammacsays@gmail.com)
To: Nick Valeriote (nvaleriote1952@sympatico.ca)
Subject: More getting started

Hi Nick,
Been up for a while. Think we should start July 6, with sessions

every day for that week including Saturday. Six sessions, two hours each afternoon. Where?

What do you think?

Sam

Sent Tues 06/23/14 8:45 AM

From: Nick Valeriote (nvaleriote1952@sympatico.ca)

To: Sam Macleod (sammacsays@gmail.com)

Subject: RE: Getting started

Hi Sam,

Just got up. Will think about this and get back to you later this morning.

Nick

Sent Tues 06/23/14 8:49 AM

From: Sam Macleod (sammacsays@gmail.com)

To: Nick Valeriote (nvaleriote1952@sympatico.ca)

Subject: More getting started

Hi Nick,

What's taking you so long? Thought you were serious about this. Think we'll need nicknames for this project. Based on your response time from now on I'll be Tigger, upbeat, anxious, and spontaneous, and you can be Eeyore, slow, careful, and unsure. Get it?

Oh yeah!

Tigger

Sent Tues 06/23/14 8:57 AM
From: Nick Valeriote (nvaleriote1952@sympatico.ca)
To: Sam Macleod (sammacsays@gmail.com)
Subject: RE: More getting started

Dear Tigger,
Okay, I get it. Can almost see you thumping around the house. You sure have a lot more enthusiasm than last night when I asked you about this.

Still need a coffee and some time. Do you ever sleep? Oh, forgot old people don't sleep much.
Back to you soon,
Oh well,
Eeyore

———————————

Sent Tues 06/23/14 9:32 AM
From: Nick Valeriote (nvaleriote1952@sympatico.ca)
To: Sam Macleod (sammacsays@gmail.com)
Subject: Getting started — location

Dear Tigger,
July 6th should be good. Six sessions packed into a week is fine. What time of day?

I see three choices for location — you decide:

The Legion hall where we were yesterday. They have some smaller meeting rooms.

The Italian Canadian Club.

My new building — means roughing it.
Eeyore

———————————

Sent Tues 06/23/14 9:36 AM
From: Sam Macleod (sammacsays@gmail.com)
To: Nick Valeriote (nvaleriote1952@sympatico.ca)
Subject: RE: Getting started — location

Dear Eeyore,

Like the idea of your building. Can you provide a place to meet afterwards and refreshments?

That's a key part of my program. I like everyone to meet and review after without me. It's important. A lot of good ideas flow out of informal discussion over a drink or coffee.

If not then I guess the Legion is the best option.

Timing should be 3:00 p.m. to 5:00 p.m. By the way I sleep as much as I ever did.

Tigger

———————

Sent Tues 06/23/14 10:33 AM
From: Nick Valeriote (nvaleriote1952@sympatico.ca)
To: Sam Macleod (sammacsays@gmail.com)
Subject: RE: Getting started — location — numbers

Dear Tigger,

My building really won't work for the social part after. I'll check the availability of the Legion.

As far as the numbers I can think of three others I can get: two guys and a lady. With me that's one more than your normal group of three — can you handle it?

Eeyore

———————

Sent Tues 06/23/14 10:41 AM

From: Sam Macleod (sammacsays@gmail.com)

To: Nick Valeriote (nvaleriote1952@sympatico.ca)

Subject: RE: Getting started — location — numbers

Dear Eeyore,

Oh I can handle it. Actually I was thinking of five this time — maybe not all seniors — a mix of those who need to work, want to try something different, and, if possible, a bucket list guy or gal who has a serious thing they're compelled to try. Can you find people like this? Actually there were some good possibilities in the audience the other day.

Don't let any of them know that we are friends or that you know me.

At least two should be women. Pick them for their ability not their looks — I know you.

Tigger

Sent Tues 06/23/14 11:10 AM

From: Nick Valeriote (nvaleriote1952@sympatico.ca)

To: Sam Macleod (sammacsays@gmail.com)

Subject: RE: Getting started — location — numbers — goals

Dear Tigger,

Let me work on getting the right people for the rest of this week. I won't grab just anyone, so I'll have to ask around, including those at your presentation. We don't have much time and we need people who fit the mold. No one I have in mind knows we're friends so I'll say this came up when I was driving you. Otherwise you were Gary's friend, so I didn't really know you. Okay?

As for goals, these are mine, what are yours?

To learn and help me make my own personal decisions about the future.

To brainstorm with you and others about possibilities.

To help you define a new webinar for people like me who need it.

Eeyore

Sent Tues 06/23/14 7:20 PM

From: Sam Macleod (sammacsays@gmail.com)

To: Nick Valeriote (nvaleriote1952@sympatico.ca)

Subject: Goals

Dear Eeyore,

Been out all afternoon. Take your time but try to get the people firmed up this week.

You know my goals are pretty lofty — encouraging the broadest possible use of entrepreneurial thinking is fairly ambitious. There is so much weight being put on entrepreneurship as the new economic wonder drug, but not enough people get why or what it really means. I'm not sure how my ideas are going to go down with seniors, even if I am one. I've been an entrepreneur my whole work life. Most people who need to be later as seniors are trying it for the first time. Old habits die hard. I'm really interested to see how this turns out — just the idea of mentoring those who should be doing the mentoring is mind boggling. Looking forward to it.

Tigger

Sent Tues 06/23/14 10:44 PM

From: Nick Valeriote (nvaleriote1952@sympatico.ca)

To: Sam Macleod (sammacsays@gmail.com)

Subject: RE: Goals

Dear Tigger,

I've booked the Legion. Small room, holds up to 20, refreshments either in the bar area afterwards or right in the room, no room charge for a home town boy. Guess they forgot what a jerk you can be.

Might have picked up one more today, another lady. If so that gives us five —three men and two women. Are you happy with that? Do you want profiles of these people in advance, or are you going to wing it? Hoping that's the case.

Eeyore

─────────────

Sent Wed 06/24/14 1:36 AM

From: Sam Macleod (sammacsays@gmail.com)

To: Nick Valeriote (nvaleriote1952@sympatico.ca)

Subject: RE: Goals

Dear Eeyore,

The mix sounds fine but no profiles. That'll be part of the first session. Trying to use some different methods on my peers, so to speak. This is new territory so I want to ask more questions at the beginning.

When we do the webinars we do a fair amount of pre-screening. This is different. First goal is to help you and maybe some other locals.

I'm tied up the rest of the week. Let's touch base Thursday. Hope you have any other details by then. I'm sure you will.

Tigger

─────────────

Sent Wed 06/24/14 6:18 PM

From: Nick Valeriote (nvaleriote1952@sympatico.ca)

To: Sam Macleod (sammacsays@gmail.com)

Subject: Goals and everything else

Dear Tigger,

Not sure when you'll get this. Had some problems with the repairs on the building today. Discouraging costs keep going up — feeling in over my head right now. Can I make this work?

Sam you've been through this many times. Is this normal? Maybe I should have just taken a job as a Walmart greeter.

Hey, maybe Gino's needs some help, seasonal work with nice fringe benefits.

I'll do my best for Thursday. Should have everything resolved by then.

Eeyore

Sent Thurs 06/25/14 2:26 AM

From: Sam Macleod (sammacsays@gmail.com)

To: Nick Valeriote (nvaleriote1952@sympatico.ca)

Subject: RE: Goals and everything else

Dear Eeyore,

I don't think you can make the grade at Gino's. You don't have what it takes to make the relish. That takes talent.

Of course you can make it work. That's what mentors are for, to make sure you do. But don't forget the old rule of thumb, the two times rule — startups cost twice as much as you project, take twice as long as you plan, and your profits will be half of what you expect. Welcome to the world of the new entrepreneur — totally outside your experience where every day is full of surprises. I used to describe a day in my first business as sitting at my desk with a revolving door into my office bringing in a constant flow of people bringing along a never ending series of problems. I thrived on it and you will too! Get with the program.

Tigger

Sent Fri 06/26/14 8:27 PM

From: Nick Valeriote (nvaleriote1952@sympatico.ca)

To: Sam Macleod (sammacsays@gmail.com)

Subject: RE: Goals and everything else

Dear Tigger,

Just watched Jeopardy. Today was a good day — I got Final Jeopardy right and all three contestants got it wrong. Always a good day when that happens.

Plus everything's under control. Other than me, the rest all look good.

Eeyore

Sent Sat 06/27/14 12:42 AM

From: Sam Macleod (sammacsays@gmail.com)

To: Nick Valeriote (nvaleriote1952@sympatico.ca)

Subject: RE: Goals and everything else

Dear Eeyore,

Maybe you should be trying out for Jeopardy as your retirement plan — could be your financial saviour.

As far as the people, maybe just confirm their ages and gender for me. No profiles, just the minimum basics. Looking forward to meeting them.

Tigger

Sent Sat 06/27/14 9:13 AM

From: Nick Valeriote (nvaleriote1952@sympatico.ca)

To: Sam Macleod (sammacsays@gmail.com)
Subject: RE: Goals and everything else

Dear Tigger,
Seriously Sam, do you ever sleep?
I've been pretty restless myself. I think I've committed too high a percentage of my resources into this building project. I guess I was focused on the potential income stream and not paying enough attention to the costs of getting it.

So for your latest escapade we have three males, ages 61, 62, and 67, plus two females aged 59 and 62. I thought I should have at least one other in their early fifties but decided against it. Is that okay? Didn't want anyone with too much energy — they might upstage me.
Eeyore

—————————————

Sent Sat 06/27/14 9:26 AM
From: Sam Macleod (sammacsays@gmail.com)
To: Nick Valeriote (nvaleriote1952@sympatico.ca)
Subject: RE: Goals and everything else

Dear Eeyore,
We're going to deal with some of your issues in the sessions — hope that'll help. In the meantime get more sleep. Every problem is magnified when you're tired. That's one lesson most entrepreneurs ignore. They push through in long hours when they really need a short break.

As for the group, five is enough. Can you ditch either the 61- or 62-year-old guy? Pick the better of the two and then find someone interesting in their early fifties. We need some diversity. Hope that's not a problem. I think you've gone too tight on the age group.

I've been getting my ideas together. This project's getting exciting. Entrepreneurship for the aged!
Tigger

Sent Sun 06/28/14 12:03 AM
From: Nick Valeriote (nvaleriote1952@sympatico.ca)
To: Sam Macleod (sammacsays@gmail.com)
Subject: RE: Goals and everything else

Dear Tigger,
The 61-year-old is definitely the better choice so I guess I stay and Mr. 62 (Don Harris) has to go.

Two glasses of wine plus an hour of Real Time with Bill Maher. Missed last night but caught just now and I'm ready to take your advice — going to bed. New rules were brutal tonight but then they generally are. Could be worse, I could be a politician. No guts no glory.
Eeyore

Sent Sun 06/28/14 12:58 AM
From: Sam Macleod (sammacsays@gmail.com)
To: Nick Valeriote (nvaleriote1952@sympatico.ca)
Subject: RE: Goals and everything else

Dear Eeyore,
Are you sure? Don Harris sounds like a good fit but I guess we *have* to keep you.

You're right about the guts before the glory. If you're going to do this you're going to have to dig deep and override some of your instincts — actually develop new instincts. Remember, prison thinking has to go. Finding the way has to become your mantra. Defining opportunities that aren't just pie in the sky ideas has to be part of it. Most of all, adjusting on the run will be your new norm. If you have to revamp your building plan to make it work, so be it. Look at other revenue possibilities and find some lower cost options to make your improvements. You can start shifting this in the right direction as early as tomorrow morning.

Taking my own advice and going to bed. One question for you: can we add one early session next week, say Thursday? I think one preview session ahead of the packed in six days will make for a better result. Can you arrange it? Can't wait to get started.
Tigger

Sent Sun 06/28/14 10:31 AM
From: Nick Valeriote (nvaleriote1952@sympatico.ca)
To: Sam Macleod (sammacsays@gmail.com)
Subject: RE: Goals and everything else

Dear Tigger,
Slept in — feel great. You're right, the problems seem less overwhelming when you're well rested.

I've had a few ideas about the building this morning. I've been on the phone for the last hour. There are things I can do to cut costs. Maybe I'll get some revenue ideas during your sessions.

Will find out about Thursday and get back to you. I don't think there'll be a problem. The Legion executives seem to like you. Not sure why. Maybe because you're so damn positive!
Eeyore

Sent Sun 06/28/14 11:10 AM
From: Sam Macleod (sammacsays@gmail.com)
To: Nick Valeriote (nvaleriote1952@sympatico.ca)
Subject: RE: Goals and everything else

Dear Eeyore,
Let me know about Thursday as soon as you find out. As for being positive, sometimes it's easier said than done, Nicky. Believe me, there are always bleak days ahead but they're not to be dwelled upon or feared. Positive thinking is critical. The power to make things happen is within us all. That's what entrepreneurs draw on when problems at any level rise up and bite them. You don't have to be a superstar to be a problem solver. All opportunities are not created equally, and only very few of us get the opportunity to be a rock star. Make the most of what you got and you'll be okay.
Tigger

Sent Mon 06/29/14 10:20 AM
From: Nick Valeriote (nvaleriote1952@sympatico.ca)
To: Sam Macleod (sammacsays@gmail.com)
Subject: RE: Goals and everything else

Dear Tigger,
Just got off the phone. We are confirmed for Thursday afternoon for 3:00. I've also added a 51-year-old guy. Surprising, actually, but you'll find out this week. Have called the other four and everyone can make it on Thursday.

So do you want me to introduce you or how do you want to start this off? I can probably find a few decent things to say if you like. All of them are excited to meet you. Not sure why.
Eeyore

———————————

Sent Mon 06/29/14 1:30 PM

From: Sam Macleod (sammacsays@gmail.com)
To: Nick Valeriote (nvaleriote1952@sympatico.ca)
Subject: Wrapping up

Dear Nick,
No more emails until this is all over in two weeks. Forget everything you know about me and just become one of the guys in the group. That's how it works best. This is the first time I've done this with a friend, but forget that friendship for now. This won't work for anyone if both of us don't do just that. I'll take it from here.
All the best,
Sam

———————————

Sent Mon 06/29/14 5:30 PM

From: Nick Valeriote (nvaleriote1952@sympatico.ca)
To: Sam Macleod (sammacsays@gmail.com)
Subject: RE: Wrapping up

Dear Sam,
Understood. Thanks again for doing this — like old times, picking teams and all.
Nick

CHAPTER SEVEN

A Fresh Start

Thursday, July 2, 2014

Sam drove out early that first afternoon so he could get a feel for the room and for the five would-be entrepreneurs, average age sixty, who would become the prototypes for his geriatric webinar. A different challenge, for sure. Not exactly the younger, more dynamic group he would have encountered when dealing with millennials.

Unknown to him, the five of us had had an impromptu meeting of our own that morning to prepare. In the heat of the moment we had dubbed ourselves the "Late Boomers," based on the fact that we were all baby boomers but were coming to the entrepreneurial trough to drink his economic elixir later in life. That pretty well summed up our attitude approaching the sessions with Sam. All of us were excited about the new opportunity and viewed Sam as the fiscal saviour who would offer the solution to our problems. Naive, of course, but even seniors need hope. Our Freedom 55 dreams had been dashed in 2008. The irony that our life expectancy had improved, taking our financial needs higher just as our resources hit the wall, was on everyone's mind.

This was not at all the end-of-life scenario we expected. We were part of the locust generation — pampered, over stimulated, and overindulged. That duly entitled age group known as "baby boomers" that had been catered to since birth, grounded in consumerism and consumption, oblivious to the needs, experience, or implications for any other generation. Our working life started in a period of ease and our retirement had long been designated to be fully funded, to start early, and to last long. Whoops! Instead we were confronted by the need to extend our usefulness and our earning power in the midst of a fast-paced world determined to shunt us aside. There was more than a little bitterness evident in our discussion that morning. But the pre-meeting had served a purpose — it was the start of a bonding process that would solidify us as a group over the next few days. Sam would be the mentor. We would be the focus.

Three men and two women; all five of us had heard Sam speak a little over a week before. The path of least resistance for me was to find recruits from that initial audience; to seek out others who were already interested in Sam's ideas. The reasons that they gave for joining in today were widespread and quite surprising. As a result I straddled a fine line, determined to be an integral part of the group as Sam had suggested while suppressing my old friendship with him in the process as I learned more about the others. It really wasn't that difficult. Despite all the Winnie the Pooh inspired repartee in our emails, my friendship with Sam was grounded in youth and nostalgia, not in the trust and loyalty earned between adults. I still worshipped Sam but I didn't really know him. In retrospect I'm not sure that anyone did. The five of us were fragile, battle weary veterans plagued by uncertainty.

First was Doris Roberts; an old friend of mine, not married, age fifty-nine, a career receptionist in a local real estate office from which both she and I had expected her career to end gracefully in a few years. It was not to be. I was surprised at her interest until this morning when she outlined a severe fracture in her life plan.

"A month ago Mr. Schneider announced he was closing the office in two months. That's all he told us; no prior indication of the change, no sale to a larger firm, no option for staff to buy him out. I knew he wanted to retire but I expected the business to continue in some form. I guess he ran out of options. He just wants the office building for a rental income and has a reliable tenant lined up. That's all. I'm not sure exactly what it means to me, but I need to work both financially and emotionally."

Next was Mayor Margaret Castlefield, age sixty-two, another unlikely candidate, a career politician who shocked us all that morning by swearing us to secrecy and announcing that she would not be running for re-election. Her interest in this group had caught me completely off guard. I'd always thought that Margaret would return to the university community and resume her career as a professor when her political career ended. She explained her reasons quite openly at our pre-meeting.

"Frankly, after almost thirty years I've lost my stomach for the whole political process. I've become a total cynic about government and bureaucracy. Plus, if I'm honest, I have a sense that I just might get thrashed if I run again. I'd rather avoid the embarrassment. I don't need the money but I have a few things left to prove. I've always wanted to try something in the private sector."

The first man in the group was Paul Groves, age sixty-seven, who had served as the on-staff accountant and a close associate of mine at my old company. We had worked together for over thirty years. Paul had accepted his golden handshake immediately, not staying around for those last two years as I had. Whenever I had seen him since, he gave the impression that his investments were doing well. That is until today. Once again I was caught off guard and was quite incredulous as he struggled to explain his interest and his needs.

"I didn't foresee that I would ever need a meeting like this. Back in 2008, at sixty-one, I was basically home free with enough assets to retire in comfort, ready to enjoy the worry-free retirement we all counted on. However, like many others I'd been seduced and held a substantial portion of my assets in equity investments, which declined with the fortunes of gold, oil, and other resource-based stocks. When I took the golden handshake almost three years ago I intended to use the funds to become a day trader but I can't pull the trigger. I've compounded the situation by losing my nerve and abandoning the market, so I missed the recovery because I've been too paralyzed to invest. There are a lot of seniors like me who lost a nest egg and pulled away from the market at the worst possible time. I've tried but I can't go back to that type of investment. I can't take that risk again. I have to find another way!"

The biggest surprise however, had happened when I began looking for someone in their early fifties to round out the group; someone with somewhat different needs than the rest of us. Paul had introduced me to Martin Goetz several years ago; now fifty-one, he was the same fellow who had spoken in such a derogatory fashion to Sam at his presentation, sceptical about the ability for big business to welcome and accept entrepreneurs within their corporate structures. Martin had contacted me a week ago with no explanation and he was still shell-shocked when the group met that morning, which showed both in his demeanour and his comments.

"A few days ago, my employer let me go. Just like that, no warning. I'm to be replaced by a much younger American from head office. What does he know about this market? What did I do wrong? I was literally escorted out of the building, given no option to phase down, just told to clean out my desk and leave. The company's going in a different direction, so I'm considered redundant. Can you believe it? After twenty-five years? Their settlement's generous, but what am I going to do? I've fired a lot of people but I had no idea what's it feels like to be on the other side of the firing line. I have no idea what I'm going to do, but whatever it is I want more control over my future. Frankly this sucks and it hurts!"

This poor man who had seemed so overconfident and more than a little self-serving a few days ago was numb and dysfunctional. He was difficult to like but I found myself feeling sorry for him. At least I could relate. I'm sure he felt that a tank had run right over him.

Last of course was me. As I watched Martin struggle I realized that I still felt the pain of going through a similar unexpected divorce. There really is no better term to describe it. One minute you're in the midst of a comfortable long-term working relationship when someone presents you with divorce papers in the form of a severance on the basis that your business partner/employer no longer wishes to continue your long-time association. Your own feelings are inconsequential. There is no room for discussion. The divorce has already been granted. I had been where Martin was now and it did suck. I don't think the hurt ever disappears. It gets buried, but periodically it resurfaces and the pain comes back. I could share his pain but unlike him and the others I had a plan. So despite my doubts, after a brief summary of my own dilemma, I put the best face on my situation that I could.

"My jolt into reality came two years ago. It has taken time to adjust but I'm confident that my rental property is going to solve most of my problems. All I need is business advice from Sam to make sure it works out."

Inside I had a nagging fear that the building might create more issues for me but there was no way I came prepared to reveal that to my new best friends. So this was the group to whom Sam brought his healing powers on that summer Thursday in July.

Right on schedule, I met with Sam around 2:00 p.m. at the Legion hall. Despite his professed disinterest in knowing things in advance, I spent the next hour giving him background information on the five of us, providing all the details I had about everyone's problems and expectations, including my own ambitious project. None of it seemed to faze him. I knew that Sam was a problem solver but hadn't realized how analytical he'd become.

As I presented each situation he asked more than enough rapid fire questions about each attendee, starting with Doris and ending with Martin.

"As I remember, Doris was far more than a receptionist. She basically ran that office. Do you think she might try to run her own show? Did she deal with customers? Does she understand real estate valuation? Did she ever work anywhere else? She has great experience but does she have the drive to start something new?

"Martin Goetz seemed intractable at the Legion meeting. Why would a guy like that want advice from me? Would he even take it? What changed his mind? How big was the corporate division that he ran? What's his reputation in town?"

In between there were numerous questions about Margaret, David, and myself. Of course I couldn't answer all of them. I was even confused about some concerning me and was sure the others would be equally off balance if asked directly. My issues were new to him and the others unknown but he said just enough to help me recognize that he was already focusing in on solutions not the problems that we were bringing to the table. I also sensed that knowing his audience was an important element in Sam controlling the situation. He was a quick study and a good thing that he was. The hour had flown by so we had barely finished the review when the rest of the group arrived.

CHAPTER EIGHT

Off and Running

There was an immediate noticeable change in the feel of the room as nervous energy pervaded the space. Fortunately it wasn't a classroom or even a traditional meeting room. The six of us sat around a large circular table more suited for a party than a seminar. Despite the informality, we five novices, a term that belied our age, were feeling a wide spectrum of emotions from foolishness to elation. I was leaning toward the latter, hopeful for a serious change in direction. Sam dove right in.

"Well it looks like we've got a fairly diverse group. Maybe we can start by going around the table and having each one of you give a one or two sentence summary of why you're here today and what you've done in the past. Let's start with Martin."

I thought that Martin's presence might throw Sam off, but he appeared determined to flush out any uncertainty up front. Martin was less anxious. After a brief hesitation the reluctant apprentice replied.

"Well, Sam, I admit I had some doubts when I heard you speak two weeks ago, especially about the receptiveness of larger companies to accept entrepreneurs as an important element of their management. This may surprise you, but after listening to you I'd decided to start promoting the idea within my company. I didn't get the chance. As of last week I'm an unemployed executive at fifty-one and entirely unprepared for it. For the past ten years I've been the general manager at Ossoff Manufacturing. We, I should say they, produce auto parts for the aftermarket sector. Until last week I expected to retire from there. With your help, I'm here to create a new me."

That set the stage. It was soon clear that we were all on the same page, determined to re-invent ourselves, or at least make a significant change in the status quo, no matter what our age and stage suggested. Paul Groves went next.

"At sixty-seven you would think my needs would be different than Martin's, but they're pretty similar. I'm still reeling from the hit my investments took back in 2008. I abandoned the market then and haven't had the nerve to go back. Now I'm burning through my assets and I'm still afraid to invest in the market. I need to find a new and better way to generate cash for the future. I worked with Nick as the secretary treasurer of Bradley Engineering, so I'm pretty well versed in financing for privately owned companies. Before my time at Bradley I was very involved in the IPO for Landis Engineering. Helping take that company public was one of my finer achievements. It doesn't mean much anymore. I feel like I've regressed twenty years and may never recover."

Sam seemed quite pensive but chose not to comment. He simply nodded to Margaret to go next. After Martin, she was the second enigma in the group and Sam wanted to know more about her motives. A true politician, she didn't hesitate at all. Talking was easy for her, but unlike most of her kind, that day she was an open book.

"If you must know, I had a sense that I couldn't get re-elected. You get pretty good at reading the voters after a few years. I'd rather go out on my own terms when I decide; getting turfed out doesn't appeal to me, so I've decided not to run in the next election. Sorry, Martin, you've reminded me why I'm not waiting for the hammer to fall. Too many politicians overstay their welcome. I've been wrestling with the decision for a while but when I heard you talk about social entrepreneurship I felt that could be my answer. People have expected so much from me and my Council cohorts over the years and lately I've realized that very few of us deliver. The system is broken; there's too much worry about getting re-elected and pleasing the press. You end up chasing your tail and completely forgetting what made you run in the first place. It's like living in the midst of comedic farce without the slapstick. You become divorced from reality, overwhelmed with lengthy staff reports and recommendations that you don't fully comprehend. Regardless, my skills are all related to politics. It's been too long since I gave a meaningful lecture without an agenda to accomplish. Opening doors is what I do best. It just seems like I can accomplish more if I become one of your social entrepreneurs, if you can help me do it."

Sam just nodded again, declining to comment, and then turned to Doris, who was the most nervous of all of us. This time the response was slower and much less certain. Just having Sam looking directly at her was enough to start the tears.

"I probably shouldn't be here. I still think of myself as a secretary. I never quite made the jump to executive assistant and I definitely didn't think that Mr. Schneider would just close down. I thought I could work there as long as I needed. What a fool! I kept hearing about people changing jobs so many times in their career but I felt safe and secure. All I really wanted was job security. Now I'm fifty-nine with no job and no idea what to do. Who wants to hire a senior secretary?"

Sam showed some empathy for Doris. No one else had elicited any sign of sympathy.

"Well, Doris, you're wrong. You're just plain wrong. You have long been an effective executive assistant, no matter what title you take for yourself. We're also going to draw out a whole range of skills that you have and a number of opportunities. So no more tears, you do belong here. In fact, all of you need to stop feeling sorry for yourselves. You need to forget apologizing for who you are and where you are because we're here to find solutions. That's all that matters."

And then it was my turn. It was easy because I had already shared my plans with Sam.

"Well, Sam, I'm well on the road to the new me. I've invested in my building and now I just need business advice to make it work as my retirement plan. That's it in a nutshell."

For the first time Sam responded to one of us with a series of questions.

"Really, Nick? It's as simple as all that? You don't have any carryover issues that have been holding you back? Your confidence hasn't been shaken like everyone else here?"

What was that about? After showing no reaction Sam had switched quickly from indifference to empathy and then to intimidation. At least that's how it felt to me. Was I being a little testy? That brief hesitation changed my response and a touch of reality overrode my denial and poured out of me.

"Maybe I have lost some confidence in my ability. I thought my dreams were within reach. I did everything I was supposed to do. My mind was already negotiating an earn out purchase of the company. I'd even started building my team with Paul as an integral member. It was the perfect scenario — I had the ability to buy the company on terms that would work and give my employer a sale so he could retire at a better price than he would otherwise get. That discussion never happened. Damn George Bradley anyway! He never gave me a chance. He just sold out to the Americans."

Sam looked more encouraging as he nodded at my comments.

"Sorry, but I had to drag that out of you. The basis of this exercise starts with a reality check. The abrupt death of a dream or a job is traumatic. All of you are still dealing with a loss — a sudden change of circumstances that had a major impact on your life. Are you familiar with the five stages of grieving: denial, anger, bargaining, depression, and acceptance?"

It seemed certain that all of us had a passing knowledge of the five stages of grief. Age ensures that grief has stepped into your personal life at some point.

"Everyone in this group is at one of these stages. That's generally the situation for seniors looking for a change. Life has thrown us a curve and we need to adjust. In that sense extending your work life is no different than compulsory retirement. It's all about change when we really don't want it. By a week from Saturday I hope to get you to stage five, acceptance, so you can move ahead. In the meantime you need to figure out where you are and what you need to move forward. Each of you needs to do your own personal SWOT analysis. What are your strengths, weaknesses, opportunities, and threats? Let's consider you as a group. How do you see your strengths? What's the biggest strength you share?"

Martin volunteered our first answer. "It has to be experience."

Sam agreed but demanded more. "Fine, but let's go deeper. What makes up the list of attributes that stem from your experience? Just shout them out."

"Judgment," said Margaret.

"Patience," added Paul.

"Management skills," I chimed in.

"Contacts, knowledge, recognition, people management, team building, sourcing, analytics, performance." All followed from various members of the Late Boomers, who were now all smiles. Of course there were others, but at that point we didn't care. The list was impressive.

Sam was also smiling.

"How does that list make you feel?"

Doris, who had not really spoken out, answered for all of us.

"It gives me confidence. Maybe we're better prepared than we think."

The negative vibes in the room had disappeared and we were engaged. Sam moved ahead, not giving us a chance to slip back into our various stages of self-doubt.

"This is good, but I promised you a reality check. So what are your collective weaknesses?"

Martin was first again.

"In some ways we know too much. Lately I've noticed that success isn't nearly as thrilling because I recognize that negatives will come. So business hasn't been as uplifting when it's going right and the thought of any downturn weighs on me. I guess I lack enthusiasm."

Sam looked at me, both of us were surprised that Martin was making such a strong contribution.

"Okay. Let's break enthusiasm down the same way we did experience. Just shout out your first thoughts about what you might be missing."

"Determination," said Paul.

"Passion," added Doris.

"Excitement and drive," Margaret added.

I knew this oh so well. I knew what had to be done to make my building a success. I'd just lacked the initiative to give it an all-out effort.

"We're all suffering from bag lady syndrome. We're afraid will lose what we've got, no matter how little that is. Even when we know we need more we're risk adverse, which suppresses our drive. That's what's been holding me back."

Everyone else looked at me in agreement. I could see it on their faces. Sam didn't want those negative thoughts to fester.

"So if the two most critical elements for becoming an entrepreneur are opportunity and determination, where do you stand?"

Martin was ready again just like the kid in class that always waved his hand frantically to give the answer and please the teacher.

"Long on opportunities and short on determination."

"That's about it," said Sam. "So what's the most critical thing you need to do?"

Doris was smiling, well over her earlier tears, "Well it would help if we were forty or fifty years younger."

"Would it?" asked Sam.

I knew the answer to that. "No, it would just reverse things. We'd be long on determination and short on opportunity."

"Exactly," said Sam. "But I have an alternative for you. It's the reason I wanted this early session, to propose a change in the setup for these sessions. With age comes experience and the ability to mentor. With youth comes passion, drive and determination, and the need to be mentored. We know which side of the equation you all come down on. I want to expand this group by the time we start on Monday. We need to get you all a transfusion of energy and enthusiasm, even a touch of naïveté will help. I need each of you to go out and find an alter ego by next Monday morning. Each of you has to find a young person who is struggling to get started and bring them to that first session next week. Let Nick know who you recruit."

CHAPTER NINE

Dining with Sam

Talk about keeping your audience off balance. None of us had expected that challenge, and most of us didn't welcome it. The Late Boomers had a quick team back after Sam ended the session. Sam had thrown us a curve. No one seemed comfortable with bringing in millennials. Everyone seemed to agree they had a questionable work ethic. Besides that somewhat natural resistance there was a little consternation about who anyone could actually bring by Monday. Overall, these concerns were in the context of a much more upbeat group than the one that had met in the morning.

While we were unanimous about feeling better it was agreed that Sam might be right; maybe we couldn't rekindle our enthusiasm on our own. Regardless, the room cleared out quickly, leaving Sam and me to do the post mortem.

I still wasn't sure I liked the latest wrinkle Sam had thrown at us, and I said so.

"I don't know if I can be mentored myself, never mind telling some overprotected young kid with no experience what he or she should do. Remember that old musical *Stop the World — I Want to Get Off*? That's exactly how I feel some days. The biggest song from that show was: "What Kind of Fool Am I?" — even more appropriate. I'm just so damn confused. Nothing has gone according to Hoyle lately. Things are changing so fast. Seriously, how is our rag-tag group of mixed up seniors going to help young people get started? And how is trying to mentor them going to help us? I just don't get it."

He was enjoying my discomfort. There was a small smirk, not quite smug, but something that said "Trust me, you're going to enjoy this." At least that's what I read into it after he spoke.

"Nick, this is just like the old days. I chose you for this team because I believe you can do it, not because I feel sorry for you. That was never the case, even when you were six years old. The first thing you have to understand is what mentoring means. I didn't come here to tell any of you what to do. We're going to work through a process and at the end you're all going to tell me what you've decided to do. And that's exactly how you're going to mentor these kids. We're going to share ideas and see where that takes us. Have some faith. Adding youth is going to increase the possibilities for both groups. You'll see."

I wasn't so sure, plus I felt compelled to defend the interest of my peer group.

"I think all of us are unsettled by the change. We feel comfortable with the group as it is. We're all in the same boat, over the hill and under-appreciated, a bunch of discards on the brink of retirement. We have nothing in common with novices trying to get started. We're a long way from being immature and carefree."

Sam was looking at me in a way that defined total disbelief. His face was red, his eyes were bulging, and the veins in his neck were protruding. He was angry! When he spoke he was close to yelling.

"Where do I start? That was quite a statement. First, comfort isn't in the cards. If you stay in your comfort zone nothing is going to come of this! Second, if you think that you're just plain done or that you're being picked on because of your age, the same goes — nothing's going to improve! Third, you're going to find out just how much you do have in common with these kids, because as I see it that's the key for all of you. Finally, you could all do with a solid dose of carefree and start enjoying life again. Besides, this is a bit of payback that I have to do."

I'd never seen Sam lose his cool. I didn't like it. He was intimidating.

"What do you mean, payback?"

He immediately reverted to his normal soft-spoken tone.

"Well Nick, you know I started out at twenty-three myself. I know what it's like. I've walked in their shoes. I can help these kids, and I should, simple as that."

I was totally confused.

"What's that got to do with payback? From what I know no one ever mentored you."

He seemed a little melancholy as he looked me right in the eye.

"That's where you're wrong, Nick. I was mentored from the grave. My father-in-law provided a road map and a wealth of contacts: customers who were patient, suppliers, who were supportive, a banker who went to bat for two inexperienced kids, and six employees who were loyal enough to stick around. We used to think we did it all ourselves but in our hearts we know better. We worked our butts off, but there was mentoring going on for sure. This is one way I can repay the debt."

What could I possibly say and do after that? Besides, I did trust him. He had a great ability to reassure people. I'd seen him do it in his webinar, even from a distance.

No more talk of that. We were off to Gino's again for the old ninety cent meal — a hot dog, onion rings, and a milkshake. At least that's what it cost in 1963. Now it was more like ten bucks, still a good deal. Along the way Sam told me that his wife, Robin, would be away next week so he was planning on staying out here to save going back and forth into the city next week. I pretty much had to offer our spare room. Thirty years of never seeing the guy and now he was practically going to be my roommate, at least for a week.

We sent most of the time kibitzing back and forth, each of us trying for one-upmanship and not quite getting it. Sam was interested in knowing more about my family. Two of my grandsons were playing on a rep football team together. I had seen them win their third game in a row the night before, so he was all ears to find out how they had played. When he found out they were playing again the following week he got super excited about going to the game with me. Then he switched back to the sessions. He'd thought of another request for me.

"Nick I think you know that one element I've always insisted on for all my seminars is that the group gets together afterward to have their own discussion. That's why I asked you to arrange for a drink after the seminars next week. Generally I stay away from those follow-up debates. I've always wanted the individuals to mold themselves into a team without me being there and forcing it. Generally this has been one of the strong points of my overall approach. Until now this has usually been coffee and doughnuts or something close to that — very informal. The idea came from the end-of-day practice my brother-in-law and I had in our first business. He always kept a large bottle of rum in his office. We called it *Cuba Libre* downtime — rum and coke was the house drink. Every day our key guys would end the day in his office or mine with the two of us to wind down, relax, and share ideas and problems that came up during the day. Often we found solutions. If nothing else it kept production, sales, and administration on the same page. Some of the best strategy came out of those informal non-meetings. Anyway, since we're meeting at the Legion I'd like to try something different at these sessions. We'll end each day with a casual drink and an open discussion, but for once I'd like to be there. What do you think?"

What did I know? This version of Sam seemed more relaxed and a little more involved than the online Sam. Not that he was aloof in his webinars. Quite the opposite, he was always approachable. Maybe because he was back at home he just wanted to try a different approach. Regardless, this all seemed fine to me, so I agreed. A drink at the end of the day worked for me. Then it was my turn to bring up an issue that was bugging me.

"How am I going to get the right mix of young people for the meeting on Monday in just three days?"

Sam wasn't much help. "Being an entrepreneur means becoming a problem solver. Three days is an eternity compared to some issues you're going to face. Start where you did the last time. There were several young people who asked questions when I spoke here last week. Start with them, but make sure they're serious. I'd rather you didn't bring anybody than show up with five bodies that are just killing time. If that happens the idea of bringing the two groups together is a bad one. Make sure everyone else knows that as well; no one settles for another warm body. I want some of these kids that are trying to get their career started and are frustrated because they can't figure out how. No pain, no gain; there has to be a willingness to make the effort. So with that in mind, you have your work cut out for you this weekend. I'd better get moving myself."

As he left, I felt good. The next week was going to be interesting. Could one week really change things that much? Time would soon tell.

CHAPTER TEN

Looking for Good Will Hunting

The search for younger talent started in earnest the next morning. It was quite the process, which had the Late Boomers using their cell phones far more than usual to contact each other, not to mention approaching any potential candidates they could identify. Each of us seemed determined to find an exceptional talent. My own fantasy, acted out in a dream the night before, involved finding an undiscovered Matt Damon–Will Hunting type with a high IQ who would become the next Mark Zuckerberg under my direction — no delusions there. None of us liked texting so that didn't help us reach out to young people who preferred to text and seldom answered a call from an unknown number. None of us were much for social media; emailing was as far as we went. No Twitter, no Instagram, no LinkedIn, even Facebook was limited to family and the odd picture. Progress was slow. By the end of the first day I was on great terms with my senior mates, but we hadn't added anyone on the junior side. It seemed that we had identified a significant item to add to Sam's list of senior's weaknesses: a complete ignorance of social media.

The only name I could recall from Sam's first appearance was Dominic, the young fellow who'd just finished secondary school but was cynical about going on. What a shame; the boy had expressed himself well, demonstrating an ability to think on his feet, even when confronted by Sam, to whom, in spite of his negative attitude, he'd shown respect. I thought he'd be a great candidate who would speak up. I also remembered him mentioning his sister who was a recent university graduate, struggling to find a job while treading water under the weight of her debt load incurred to earn her degree. If I could just find them I'd try for both. Her frustration was exactly the element Sam wanted to bring to the group. He and I had discussed the dilemma facing our grandchildren. Young people were facing serious barriers that were preventing them from jump-starting their careers. Education was proving to be no guarantee of opportunity. Many recent graduates were taking lower-level jobs just to survive. Too many were forced to go back to living with their parents. It was a concern, and no solution seemed to be on the horizon.

On Saturday afternoon I tracked down an old friend, Ron Hayward, at the grocery store that he managed. Since he employed a lot of students he was tied in to the teen network, which was why I'd gone to see him. When I asked, it turned out that he knew Dominic pretty well.

"You came to the right place. I know Dominic and his parents. You remember George Martini, Gerry's younger brother? He's Dominic's father. He and his wife live down on River Road with a bunch of kids, four, maybe five. I think Dominic's right in the middle. A good kid. He restocks shelves for me and he'll be in tonight around 8:00 if you can come back."

Finally, a break! But when I did go back Dominic wasn't interested.

"Sorry, Mr. Valeriote, I really don't see how this is going to help me. I have to make up my own mind. I've got acceptance at two universities and three colleges but I'm afraid of the debt. My parents want me to go but I have to borrow. With three other kids at home they can't help. My sister Andrea graduated a year ago and right now she's stuck with big debt and a job waitressing. That's all she can get. Maybe you should talk to her."

All I could hear in my head was Sam's voice saying "solve the problem," and this *was* a problem. I didn't want to see this kid squander his future without getting better exposure to his options. I wanted him in those group sessions. Somehow I had the sense that his presence would even help me. What to do? First change the subject and buy some time to think.

"How did you feel about Sam Macleod's ideas? I was there when you asked your question."

Dominic didn't hesitate. "He was all right; more in touch with our problems than most."

A glimmer of hope! Perhaps a carrot would help.

"Well Sam's running this group. We started with seniors only but he's insisting that we add some young people. It's only one week of your time during the day so it won't interfere with your work here. Look, I'm no different than you. I'm trying to get restarted just like you're trying to get started for the first time. Maybe we can help each other. What do you say?" I could tell that I'd sparked some interest, so I pressed on. "Maybe you could get Andrea to come as well."

There were actually tears in his eyes at the thought.

"I'd really like to help Andrea. She's been so worried. My parents are worried. That's why I'm afraid to go on myself. We both need some guidance from someone like Mr. Macleod. I'm pretty sure I can get her to come."

Just like that I had not one but two recruits and beat my quota. Dominic was eighteen, Andrea was twenty-two. Two different stages and two different genders, both would be good additions. It felt great.

By Sunday afternoon we had two more. First Margaret Castlefield called. She had managed to convince her grand-daughter Hannah to join the group. Hannah was a twenty-three-year-old graduate student with an engineering degree. She was interested in startups and had heard about Sam. A few minutes later Martin Goetz called me. Since his unexpected dismissal he'd decided to take some time off to sort things out, but in the short term he had decided to throw himself into a major cleanup/ redecoration at his house. In the middle of the first job he realized that he couldn't do much by himself so he'd hired his neighbour's son to help him for the next month or two at minimum wage. Reluctantly he admitted he'd picked an unemployed young guy rather than a handyman to save money. After the first day he was impressed with the young man's work ethic and they'd become friendly enough for Martin to mention our sessions with Sam. It seemed that twenty-four-year-old Jake Oldfield wanted to run his own business. By the end of the day Martin had convinced him to work mornings with him next week and to join our group in the afternoons.

With some degree of relief I fired off an email to Sam giving him what information I had about the four additions. The answer was short but effective, reinforcing my sense of satisfaction.

"Eeyore: Better than expected. Problem solved. See you tomorrow. Tigger."

CHAPTER ELEVEN

Finding Symmetry

Sam was late. He arrived at my house around 2:30, leaving us little time to talk beforehand. Once I confirmed that we were all set for the after session he didn't say much. On the way over to the Legion he admitted that blending the two age groups together was a risk and his biggest concern. At this point it was an uncontrolled experiment and Sam was outside his comfort zone.

"I'm used to fairly likeminded groups with common goals. If I can't establish the commonality right away, we won't get far with this new approach. On the surface these two groups are competing for space in a declining labour market. Early exit for seniors means opportunity for youth, while extending careers for seniors who need to work but are less ambitious clogs up entry-level positions for new graduates. There is a resentment factor, and that's the hurdle we have to clear today."

That's all he would say. The rest of the drive over was silent.

We arrived to find everyone there, but sitting at two different tables, divided by age — not encouraging. Even Hannah had opted to sit with the other young people rather than her grandmother. Both groups were busy talking as we arrived. Sam went right over and introduced himself to the newcomers before calling the session to order. The first thing he did was change the layout, integrating the group in the process.

"Don't get too comfortable with your peers. We're going to change this up. I want all of you sitting in a semi-circle, alternating by age group. Let's get moving — we only have six days and a lot to accomplish."

The shuffling around only took a minute. Sam decided not to put the newcomers on the spot. Since I'd explained on our walk from the car that we'd recruited them under some duress, he let them off easy with no explanation why they had come. He'd been wrestling with that on the way over in the car, asking my opinion at the last minute. When we hit the parking lot he still hadn't decided how to break the ice. No one else had any sense of his hesitation. He was the picture of confidence as he started by having us shake hands with the people on either side. Then he moved right into high gear.

"Two weeks ago none of you had any plans to be here. As of last Friday four of you still didn't. Normally I don't recruit, individuals with problems come to me. My groups are always small and are made up of people facing very similar circumstances. On the surface this is a grand experiment involving more people than usual from two very different and easily distinguished groups. On the surface you seem to have completely opposite problems causing you to compete for scarce opportunities. I understand that our second group was almost coerced to be here and I'm confident that at this moment each of you is questioning why you agreed. However, that's not the way I see it. Your differences can become your strength. By the end of today I intend to convince you that your two subsets are natural allies who through co-operation have the ability to multiply the opportunities for all."

As he sipped from his ever-present bottle of water, I had to admit that he had everyone's attention, albeit punctuated by a series of questioning looks.

"I'm not going to spend time defining entrepreneurship or giving you a crash course in the basics. I have a complimentary copy of my book here — a simple book on a complex subject, written as a narrative, filled with common-sense advice in terms anyone can understand. I expect you to read part of it each night and complete it before our last session on Saturday. It should encourage you, introduce you to a whole range of business fundamentals for entrepreneurs, and prepare you for what's ahead. What it won't do is deal with your unprecedented circumstances. We all live and work in a global economy that is moving at warp speed. At the moment we're in the midst of an economic world in transition, compounded by the fact that there's a decline in the demand for labour due to technological innovation and an increase in the supply due to globalization. That hits the labour force particularly hard at the shoulder points, exactly where all of you sit, either fighting to enter the labour force or struggling to hang on, not quite ready to leave. Whether starting up or winding down, all of you are on the fringe and facing hurdles. In simple terms on an individual level, we're operating in an economy characterized by barriers to entry and predispositions to force people out prematurely — delayed entry and forced exit. Sound familiar?

"I will offer up my own simple definition of entrepreneurship, which many of you heard if you came to see me two weeks ago. That word is *self-determination*. In the face of your limitations the best option for all of you is to take control. That's the first thing you have in common. You've already heard me say this and you'll hear me say it over and over: the most important skill to learn today is the ability to create and manage your career. It doesn't matter at what age or stage you acquire that skill. What matters is that you do! Don't become a victim, get ahead of the curve!

"So that's my overview. Now I want to talk about some specifics and your perceptions of each other at the outset. Starting with the seniors, lets list their strengths first followed by their weaknesses. We'll just go along the semi-circle, starting with Paul on the left. One strength from each of you."

By the time each of us had had their turn we had produced the following list with the even numbered responses coming from the newcomers:

1. Contacts
2. Experience and judgment
3. Work ethic
4. Declining financial needs, increasing staying power
5. Willingness to work for equity
6. Access to funds
7. Exposure to market opportunities
8. Networking, including professional advisors, customer base, and key suppliers
9. Maturity

"Not bad," said Sam. "Fairly comprehensive. Now let's do the same for weaknesses, starting where we finished with Doris."

This time we produced the following list:

1. Knowledge of technology
2. Activity on social media
3. Risk adverse
4. Lack of passion
5. Resistant to change
6. Close minded to new ideas, new products, and new approaches
7. Short-term focus
8. Lack of respect for millennials
9. Less willing to travel or put in long hours

Sam seemed relatively pleased with this as well.

"There's a pattern developing reflecting how you perceive each other and yourselves. Overall it seems that our 'seniorpreneurs' have many attributes that could create opportunity while being risk adverse and a bit light on some of the characteristics needed to capitalize on those same opportunities. Let's see what you think about our 'youthpreneurs,' starting with Paul again on their strengths."

We were catching on, so in short order we had produced the following list:

1. Drive and passion
2. Willingness to take risk
3. Technological knowledge
4. Social media networking
5. Adaptability, resilience, and openness to learn
6. Willingness to put up sweat equity through long hours, travel, and low pay
7. Knowledge of current trends within an era of change
8. Productivity
9. Long-term focus

Sam was smiling but without any discussion asked Doris to start the last list — weaknesses of the youth group.

1. Lack of experience
2. No business network
3. Very limited access to funds
4. Lack of market exposure
5. Limited knowledge of business practice and fundamental business issues
6. No professional network
7. Undeveloped judgment
8. Limited staying power
9. Ability to accept advice/work ethic

Sam made the initial comment. "We're not going to debate this. I'm interested in your perceptions, right or wrong. Overall there's some duplication in what you've put down, but these are fairly comprehensive lists. Maybe not definitive, but meaningful. The difference seems to be that our youth group is much longer on attributes that will allow anyone to capitalize on opportunity, such as energy and drive, but less likely to find or identify serious prospects. So would anyone like to comment on what you've produced?"

As usual, Martin was anxious to get in the first comment.

"What surprises me is that there's not much overlap on the strengths."

Dominic spoke next, apparently over some of his rookie nerves and he impressed me with his insight.

"What really strikes me is that if you merge the two into one list, most of the weaknesses are covered off within the amalgamated group. As Mr. Goetz just pointed out, the combined lineup has many more strengths and very few weaknesses, from what I can see, because what one group lacks the other covers off. I would guess that the chance of success by merging the two is much higher."

Sam was ecstatic.

"Bingo! How old did you say you are Dominic? You just nailed the closing argument. By the way, since we're in this process together we only use first names. Both you and Martin are right, but you hit the nail on the head. Individually both of these demographics have some glaring weaknesses, but once they're merged we have a team that's much closer to a complete package, maybe even a real powerhouse. That's the essence of my message for the week. Any specific age group will lack intensity in one or more areas, generally their determination may decline as they gain experience. By building a team of extremes we maximize what we can bring to the table. Your groups can't compete with each other. Depending on the issue or opportunity one will have a distinct advantage over the other but neither will bring anywhere close to the optimum approach that is possible. But once blended together you come much closer to covering all the bases. What we need to find this week are effective means to build teamwork among individuals that on the surface are so fundamentally different. Can you work together? That's the real challenge."

I checked around the room. The reaction was a mixture of enthusiasm and doubt with the split coming more or less along gender lines. Martin, Dominic, and Paul all seemed somewhat excited. Doris, Margaret, and Hannah were more subdued. Andrea looked doubtful. I was pretty happy, even optimistic, while Jake just looked bored.

Sam didn't allow us much time to reflect, preferring to get some feedback.

"So now it's time for your questions and comments."

Eager to beat Martin, I rushed in with a question without much thought.

"So are you trying to say that we *have* to partner up with millennials to succeed?"

Sam looked annoyed, expecting more from me than a quick and dirty conclusion.

"Of course not, Nick. All of you can find ways to succeed. Probably the older group has the biggest advantage because they should find opportunity, and given their needs they usually define success at a lower level of achievement. They don't have to build huge scalable businesses to reach their goals. In fact the age group that is currently starting more businesses than any other is the fifty-five- to sixty-four-year-old category because they need to, but even more because they can. So the urgency to merge is not the point and it's not essential. What I'm trying to show is that the chances of success improve and the degree of success increases when you bring people with very different abilities together. It's classic team building, but also thinking outside the box about who you recruit."

This prompted a quick reaction from Hannah.

"I'm glad you mentioned team building. Isn't this just the basic argument for teamwork? I've actually read your book. My grandmother gave it to me. You strongly promote the need for teamwork for any entrepreneur. I believe the whole idea is to have the courage to add people to your team who have strengths that you lack. How do your comments today relate to us any more than for any entrepreneur in the startup stage, regardless of age?"

Sam hesitated. I knew he was glad to be getting pushback from the youth faction. He'd expected some resistance from them.

"Thanks for reading the book. As for your question, this is definitely about teamwork and how you build your team. You're right, that's a major requirement for anyone to succeed as an entrepreneur, but this relates even more to the age groups represented here because your failings are in the area of intangibles and are more glaring, yet completely opposite. The barrier to youth right now is opportunity. The limitation for seniors is resilience. To build teams with the greatest chance of success, each of you needs to find complementary strengths, which reside in a dominant basis within the other group. You'll be hard-pressed to address these shortfalls if you follow the natural tendencies and stay within your peer group."

Martin had waited long enough. He was fresh from managing a mix of ages and had strong opinions.

"I don't think we can work together. We're two generations apart and the gap between generational thinking is increasing. I've hired millennials. They just don't see the world the way we do. The work ethic thing is a real concern. They are great at social media but they can't ignore it during the work day and that hurts productivity."

Sam was ready for that comment.

"Tell me, Martin, was your problem that millennials were less productive than their older counterparts or was it that they could have been more productive in their own right?"

Martin appeared uncomfortable. I was concerned that he might upset the newcomers.

"Well, to be honest their tech know-how saved their jobs as far as I was concerned. In the tech area they outperformed everyone else, even while distracted off and on with their social media connections. I guess you're right. The results were there but they could have accomplished more."

Sam wanted to drive the point home.

"So from what you're saying they follow a different path to a good result, is that it? In the future, when you pick your team in an organization that you own and lead, are you more interested in methods or results?"

Most of us were smiling at that point, reunited in our thinking after a potentially divisive subject.

Martin chuckled as he nodded.

"You got me Sam. I definitely want results. I guess I can learn to be tolerant about methods."

I felt I should add another comment from observing my grandchildren.

"It's not just results Sam. Methods are changing. Big Data has far reaching implications and our generation isn't well equipped for most of them. The millennials are."

Doris had a question, but not for Sam. She turned to Andrea.

"Neither of us has said much. Do you think you could work with someone like me in a new company, or do you think I'm just a throwback to another era?"

Andrea was caught off guard. I could relate. She was a listener like me who preferred to weigh their words carefully.

"Do you think you're a throwback or can you make a contribution that I'll respect?" It was usually safe to deflect a question by asking one.

Doris was smiling.

"Well, my dear, I came here full of self-doubt. But I like the lists we put together. I think I can contribute and I bet you and

I could feed off of each other and accomplish a lot between us. I know I can help you, and I could also use your help."

Andrea held out her hand and the two shook on it — progress. That seemed like a good place to end, so Sam stepped in to wind up the first session.

"While Team Oldest was recruiting Team Youngest this weekend I was busy myself. I think Nick has explained that we're going to have a short happy hour after our sessions this week. Don't worry Dominic, it's limited to one drink and it's on me. It's a good way to debrief and share ideas. I won't make you late for work. Anyway, I've arranged for different people to come in every day to share some experiences. Today we have Donovan Smiley, the founder of Student Decorators. I've known Donovan since he was twenty-two, about three years after he founded the company. He should be here in about five minutes, so get yourself a drink and relax and please share your thoughts on our discussion. Not with me, but with each other."

CHAPTER TWELVE

The Painting Guru

Donovan Smiley was a charmer, a Jamaican-born Canadian with just a touch of the accent of the islands. Older than expected, closing in on fifty, he was a sharp dresser who effused anything but students and house painting, the two things for which his company was known. I wasn't sure how he and Sam had connected but I did know he started his company very young and now it had outlets nationwide, primarily employing university students. Sam was just finishing his introduction as the rest of us, drinks in hand, settled in, eager to hear Donovan's story.

"Thank you, Sam. It's great to be here with you today. What Sam didn't mention is that after my initial success with the company I went to him for advice. He's been a key member of my advisory board ever since. He actually helped me put the board together and that's been a major contributor to our growth.

"So how did I get started? Well, like many businesses mine started out of a problem. After my first year at university I was desperate to find a summer job. There were very few jobs that year, either seasonal or for new graduates. Sound familiar? My parents wanted to help me but I knew that it would really put a strain on their budget if I couldn't pay my own way. After a week of looking long hours and applying anywhere that would take my application I was nowhere. My dad had an idea. We lived in an older clapboard house in Rexdale that needed to be painted every five years or so. That was the year and he offered to pay me to do it. He allowed me two weeks and offered me eight hundred dollars to do the job. I knew nothing about painting but I soon found that I liked the work.

"Before I knew it I was going to the library, reading every do-it-yourself book on painting that I could find. After I finished the outside I convinced my parents that the entire inside of the house needed doing and at my rate they could afford it. My mother did the wall papering since my dad didn't have the patience for it. So she became my mentor on that challenge. We did two rooms together without a disagreement and I learned the essential wallpaper mantra from her: 'measure twice cut once.' As you probably know, word of mouth advertising is the most cost effective, particularly for any service involving home improvement. By the time I finished my parents' house I had enough contracts to fill out the summer and to work Saturdays all winter long. I didn't really have a business but I was self-sufficient, independent, and in control of my short-term future. The only investment I needed was a good step ladder and the right type of brushes.

"As the winter went on I found that I was quoting more and more jobs for the upcoming summer. The quoting process was taking a long time, and I soon realized that I couldn't possibly do all the work by myself. I hated to turn down jobs, so a few things happened. First, I raised my rates by 25 percent and found no resistance. Second, I streamlined the quoting process and developed a quote form that is still the basis for what we use today. Third, I started recruiting other students and came up with the name Student Decorators. The fact that I could do wallpapering distinguished us from other student painters, who generally stayed with outside work. Once I had some potential employees I started working on a training program based on all the things I'd read. That second year I supervised all of the jobs myself with four employees working under my direction. The third year I hired two of them back to be supervisors so we had three crews.

"By this time I could see that I had a formula developing. If I trained properly I could develop supervisors for the next year and expand our volume. I also learned quickly that the biggest issues were doing the jobs on time and avoiding mistakes that required us go back to fix them. This is around the time I met Sam. We created an advisory board that included a recently retired professional painter. With the help of the board I put together an incentive plan. Every day we finished a job early the painters got a 5 percent bonus, so two days early made a 10 percent bonus. It worked for me because it didn't cost me anything. I was paying for less time on the job than budgeted. That also put the onus on me to quote properly. I had to be tight enough to get the work but there had to be opportunity for the painters to outperform my estimate and make a bonus. Secondly, any work that had to be redone was not paid. In other words, the painters paid for their mistakes by doing any repairs on their own time, which gave them the incentive to do things right in the first place. These two elements are still the cornerstones of our reward system. Our managers are pressured to quote accurately and fairly while our painters are motivated to do it right the first time.

"As we grew we expanded into different communities and we started hiring managers in each, making them responsible for securing the work, hiring, and training the crews in their area and so on. Basically doing what I did initially in their area under the umbrella of the Student Decorator name. We've expanded into cleaning services but still focus mainly on the decorating business, with many repeat customers that find jobs for us each year. We are now operating in all ten provinces, employing full-time regional managers as well as marketing and administrative staff.

We're also tied in with the placement services in every university and college in the country as part of our recruiting program. The most important ingredient is repeat customers who come back over and over as well as recommending us to others. They are the strongest marketing tool, and word of mouth is the best reference, just as it was when I was doing my parents' house. And I guess that's about it. I could use my one drink now."

Sam was on his feet and handing Donovan a glass that looked like it contained Scotch.

"That's quite a story Donovan, and like many success stories it all seems so obvious now. But it's not and it never was. This is a classic example of taking a need that exists and doing it different and better than anyone else. Being an entrepreneur does not mean being an innovator or inventor. More often than not it's about finding a different way. Young people doing odd jobs for the summer is as old as it gets but you've found a better way by thinking outside the box. It's a great example for old and young alike. Thanks so much for sharing it with us today."

We all stayed around for half an hour or so. All nine of us had a chance to speak with Donovan privately for a few minutes. The young people were respectful, but you could see he had inspired them. The comment that most stuck in my mind came from Jake, who hadn't said anything else all day.

"I've been doing jobs like that for two years and I never saw the potential. I never got out of the starting blocks. I was stuck on the idea that I was staying afloat, looking for something better, never thinking I could make more of what I was doing. I just keep thinking the future's all tied to tech, not down in the trenches doing basics."

"Nice to know that you can actually talk Jake," Sam said. "I hope you'll do more of it tomorrow. Don't worry about the past. One of the things we're working on this week is helping all of you to identify opportunity. We're surrounded by it, you know, but most of the time we're too busy to notice."

Definitely food for thought. Sam was constantly stoking the fire of ideas. Could we learn to do the same on our own?

By that time happy hour was over. Sam was strict about that. The whole concept focused on the dialogue, not the drinking, so every day that week we broke up dutifully after an hour. That night and every other that week Sam and I went home together but we spent each of those nights revitalizing a friendship. We never discussed the sessions; his rule, not mine.

CHAPTER THIRTEEN

Finding Inspiration

The next afternoon all ten of us arrived early, but once again Sam and I were the last, a precedent that we maintained all week. Sam had spent the morning on his own driving around town visiting some of his old haunts. Our discussion the night before had triggered memories that needed revisiting, which I recognized he wanted to do on his own. Whether that distraction was the reason or not, he started the second session in a wistful manner.

"I hope you enjoyed Donovan's story. We hear so much about the success of the superstars but moderate successes for people whose circumstances are much like our own don't get discussed enough. Donovan was just like you before he started: lacking opportunity, in desperate need of cash, and unsure of his ability. We need to celebrate the successes of the average instead of spending our time talking about billionaires. We might have a few Donovan types right here, but it's extremely unlikely that we have anyone like Zuckerberg, Jobs, or Gates. Well we do have a Goetz, but it's spelled differently. It's credible to aspire to match what Donovan has accomplished. Not easy, but credible. You know that it's possible; it's doubtful that any of you could have developed Facebook but most of you could learn to paint. What struck you the most in hearing his story yesterday?"

Martin was ready to rumble and jumped right in accordingly.

"I was impressed with his work ethic but very surprised by the analytical skills he used at a young age to recognize his model early on and address some very important issues, like what was critical to his customers and setting meaningful and achievable incentives for his painters. From the outset he kept his eye on the market and started building teamwork. Textbook, straight out of your book, which I read last night. No wonder you brought him here the first day."

Sam made no comment. Andrea spoke next.

"What struck me was that he liked the work himself. If he hadn't enjoyed painting his parents' house I seriously doubt that Student Decorators would exist."

"Not only that," said Jake, "he did all the jobs himself; first the painting, then the wallpapering, then crew boss, right up the ladder to the top where he sits today. That blew me away. I'm pretty confident he could still go out and paint houses today and meet the standards. Setting the right example was and is an important part of his success."

Not everyone was enthralled with Donovan. It seemed Margaret had concerns about the program.

"I liked Donovan well enough, but I thought this group started with the idea of helping seniors reinvent themselves. It seems we've switched gears and shifted all the emphasis to the young newcomers. I wish them every success, but I'm not sure how this is helping me."

Doris came to Sam's defence before anyone else could.

"Let's give this more time, Margaret. I'm here for similar reasons to you. I think Donovan's message about recognizing opportunity is important for all of us, not just the young people here. Sam is trying to build bridges and I want to see how that works out."

Apparently Paul agreed.

"I spent all of last night mulling over things that I've done in the past and thinking about needs that I can identify in my own community. I feel like I'm starting to get the gist of this. I'm with Doris — we're just getting started. Age has nothing to do with opportunity. If anything we have more options. Donovan's story motivated me to look rather than ignore."

Hannah had a mixed opinion, loyal to her grandmother but receptive to the ambition and achievements of a young person to whom she could relate.

"I kind of agree with my grandmother, but I also remember what Sam said yesterday about finding common ground. As Martin pointed out, there are great lessons in Donovan's story for all of us. I really liked the way he went about building his team and providing for their success, ensuring his own in the process. I doubt that Sam can bring in the perfect model of what our two age groups can achieve working together, but I want to know more."

As the originator of the idea for this program I felt obligated to speak up.

"Donovan was great but only our first visitor. Clearly his story has made all of us think, which I think is what Sam was looking for — thought provoking content and discussion. Now we need to move on to the next phase. What do you have in mind for today Sam? I for one can hardly wait."

Dominic was the only one of the nine who didn't comment, which seemed out of character for one that usually expressed his opinions strongly. Whatever the reason I noticed he was acting rather subdued today. Regardless Sam had a story in mind and he moved on.

"I woke up early this morning. I often do when I'm in the middle of a dream that's so real that my emotions are running high. My dreams are almost always about a problem, one that I need to fix because that's what I do: I'm a fixer. I suppose that's why I'm here. Anyway, this morning my dream was about India. I've been there ten times, always on business. In my dream I was struggling to help this brilliant eight-year-old boy that

I'd met who was saddled with supporting his family. Let's call him Sanjay. I've never met anyone that young who is quite like Sanjay, a born little salesman who exuded confidence, resilience, and determination, against all odds. He was full of personality with an amazing sense of humour and an understanding of the subtleties of life that belied his age. No matter what I tried to do I couldn't help him. Every offer I made, every opportunity I found for him, all were thwarted by some powerful third-party antagonist, my unseen enemy in the dream, who I could never seem to conjure up or put a face on. This is a recurring dream that I have that always ends with me leaving and Sanjay calling after me to take him with me.

"Sanjay's story is one that haunts me. You see, I did actually meet him. I did much of my business in India in Chennai, formerly Madras. On my second trip there, on a Sunday that I had free, my agent drove me out along the coast of the Indian Ocean, south of the city. The beaches were beautiful, far beyond my expectations for India. One of the highlights of the day was a visit to the sight of the Shore Temple at Mahabalipuram built in the eighth century right on the shore of the Bay of Bengal. It's the sight of an ancient historic town and is one of the oldest Hindu temples still standing. As we were getting out of the car to approach the temple we could see a rush of various peddlers selling souvenirs: models of the temple, small statues of the god Vishnu, and so on. Many of them were adults, but quite a few were kids. My guide admonished me not to look at them, making it clear that if I even eyeballed the merchandise, or worse, actually talked to them, they would hound us incessantly until we left. I did as I was told and as I wandered around ignoring their very existence. Most of them abandoned us in search of better prey — all but one. That was Sanjay, although I still don't know his real name. Regardless, his face is etched in my memory. Sanjay did not give up, but followed along, patiently waiting for me to make the first move — no harassment, just a charming smile.

"Of course I took the bait and spoke to him. Once engaged in conversation I found that this eight-year-old was quite possibly as good as any adult salesman who ever worked for me in any of my companies. He knew the history of the temple and the area as well as any scholar. By the end of the conversation I had purchased the 'very best' quality miniature of the temple and had offered him a job as a salesman in Canada when he grew up. He was one of the most interesting people I met in India, although there were many others, but that's another story.

"So why does Sanjay haunt my dreams? It's simple really. He represents a problem that I can't solve. There is so much talent in the world, so many potential entrepreneurs who are suppressed because of lack of education, circumstances of birth, gender, race.... the list of barriers and limitations is both long and effective. If I could I would lift all of those obstacles and turn all of these potential problem solvers free to perform. Entrepreneurs find solutions. They are the economic catalyst that puts all other resources to work. Sanjay was one. I knew it when I met him and I felt a common bond with an eight-year-old who would never get the opportunity that I've had.

"That's one reason why I have high hopes for social entrepreneurship. Bill and Melinda Gates are setting the bar high, showing that committed individuals can solve societal problems better and less costly than governments. I hope I can help Margaret in her goal of pursuing some form of social entrepreneurship to make up for her career in politics. Sorry, Margaret, but I would have you sacrifice your political wherewithal to achieve true social reform, regardless of the forum. I will never forget Sanjay, but in my wildest dreams I meet him again as an adult who runs a multinational corporation. The less credible part of the dream is meeting him. The ability to lead was already within him."

At that point there were a few chuckles at Margaret's expense. The first sounds since Sam started his story.

"Just kidding, Margaret, but there is a message in my story for all of you that no matter how deprived and denied you may feel, you have the opportunities that Sanjay may never get. You can do what Donovan has done in your own way, in your own niche, and it doesn't have to be tech related. It can be a basic bread and butter idea right out of the traditional mainstream economy. Whenever you have doubts, misgivings, or setbacks and are thinking of giving up I want you to remember Sanjay tracking me around those ruins when everyone else had given up, determined to make a sale, and getting it."

Message delivered. There was no excuse for any of us to be cynical about our prospects. His next statement was a complete non sequitur, as Sam turned his attentions toward Dominic.

"So, Dominic, have you been reading my book?"

That caught everyone off guard, particularly Dominic.

"I have, sir. It's a little intimidating. Not the story, sir, I like that. There's just so much to learn. Maybe I'm not ready for this entrepreneur thing yet."

Sam had no intention of letting this self-doubt fester. He had seen it many times before.

"For starters, don't be put off by Martin's comments about the book. You're coming at this challenge from different directions and neither of you have it quite right. Things will not come as easy as Martin thinks or nearly as hard as you feel they will right now. Martin has the advantage of experience and many of the concepts that feel foreign to you have been part of his everyday life as a manager. On the other hand he's coming from a culture of structure and control. You're starting with a clean slate, no presumptions and no bias. It's not the disadvantage that you think right now. There are few things more powerful than an open mind. You can start by embracing your doubts. What you're feeling are simply internal warnings that trigger closer examination. Fears offer the same warnings. Together they are the tools of defining and taking managed risk as opposed to reckless risk.

"All of these feelings are part of the ongoing personal SWOT analysis that every one of us needs to carry out regularly. Circumstances change and are changing at a much faster rate. Doubts will make you realize needs. They are the key to building your team as a way to reduce risk and address weaknesses. They offer the motivation to dig in your heels and find solutions. Without doubt we become gamblers who can hit it big, but more often than not fail. Without doubt none of us would do downside planning, making us less prepared and less resilient. Without doubt we would likely choose to plod ahead, feeling in total control, without delegating and with less control than we realize. Fear of failure is one of the strongest possible motivations. But as natural as doubt is, it must always be shifted to the sidelines. It is only a tool to identify problems. Once we isolate the problems determination has to take the lead. Every entrepreneur approaches his problems with a strong dose of certainty. Those problems will be solved. The exercise is about 'how,' it is never about 'if.' This is the mindset of an entrepreneur, who, by definition, *makes things happen!* That's the message you need to take away from my book, Dominic. Once you grasp that you are an entrepreneur and can move ahead with confidence. Does that make sense?"

The look on Dominic's face was one of total relief. No answer was required and Sam didn't wait for one.

"I'm glad that all of you are reading the book. We only have a few days and I need you to be up to speed on the basics. By all means ask questions here about the book, but in these brief sessions we need to focus on opportunity. All successful entrepreneurs manage to find opportunity, some more easily than others. All ideas are not opportunities and all opportunities are not created equal. Right now each one of you is dealing with entrepreneurship of necessity. Whether starting your career or extending it, you need to get results now. That may mean taking on something that's less than perfect. If you keep waiting for the perfect opportunity many others will pass you by and it may never come. So, as the song says, love the one you're with. In other words, if there's time pressure, make the most of what's available, particularly today where change is inevitable, nothing lasts forever, and every entrepreneur needs an end game. The best opportunity you have today may only be a platform leading to the real opportunity you are seeking, but take the plunge and get started. He who hesitates can indeed become lost. No one learns in a vacuum. If you are one of our seniors you don't have the time to be overly selective. If you are a junior you need experience. The perfect opportunity is an illusion, one you can't afford to wait for.

"So now I'm going to retract one statement. You know that I feel that the dialogue on entrepreneurship is far too dominated by tech talk; terms that are a by-product of the venture capital world where getting to market early is essential. Fast and furious is ingrained in the whole approach. In the traditional economy there is usually room for more patience often sustained by bootstrapping which means living within your means. However, for both groups here there is a sense of urgency and a lack of time. Finding ways to accelerate are critical so that needs to be part of your approach. In that sense you do have a common bond with the techies.

"Tomorrow we're getting into more specifics, but today I would like each of you to name one area of the economy or one industry that you feel has more upside than others, either because it's going to boom or because there are important problems to solve. Let's start with Doris and keep moving around the semi-circle. Please give us a one or two sentence explanation as well."

Doris only knew one market segment and that's what she mentioned.

"Real estate, from selling it to creating it through land development, is a localized market and a critical resource."

I think that's what Sam expected her to say.

Next was Margaret. "Well, I'm interested in social entrepreneurship, so with that in mind I'd say education. It's a critical sector that needs to change. Costs are too high but it's a mistake to cut funding in an area that is the key to our competitive advantage. Governments will not solve this. There needs to be both professional and public engagement to find solutions."

Hannah was sitting next to her grandmother. "I've been working with an incubator at the university. Lack of funding is a critical issue for startups, and startups are critical for economic growth and diversity. I see some potential with crowdfunding to engage individual investors and raise funds for startups. With that in mind I'll say finance. I know it's dominated by big players, but I think there's room for innovation."

Paul was beside her and I had overheard them talking about crowdfunding earlier. "I have sort of a similar reaction to Hannah's. I'm an accountant and I think there's opportunity for independent financial advisors like myself, whether with funding or basic management tools like knowing and understanding your key financial numbers. I like the idea of mentoring in this area. I see consulting as a growth industry for sure, and for me that means in the area of finance."

Jake was next. He was much more engaged in the discussion today. "My parents keep telling me that elder care is a growth field. That makes sense to me. I used to think they just wanted to make sure that I take care of them, but I realize the needs are growing, and aging affects most families. No offense to anyone here, but many boomers are retiring. The demographics dictate that the geriatric market will need lots of attention."

Martin had been patient, but as usual he was anxious to present his idea. "I agree with Hannah. Real growth is going to come from startups. I know from my company that it makes sense for large organizations to horde cash and grow through acquisition, buying proven ideas and technology rather than developing them. I'm not quite sure what this means to me, but as a career manager I want to help accelerate startups. I mean by playing an active role, not just being a passive investor. There's serious potential for high returns by building and selling in a short time frame. I know that's not an industry, but it's a critical trend."

Dominic had only just moved on from his doubts so I wondered if he had any concrete ideas. "My suggestion is the service industry. Donovan showed us that there are limitless possibilities if you focus on a different and better way to provide services. Anything related to maintenance and repairs or redecorating, installation, or in the case of electronics, teaching. Fundamental services for which there's a widespread need. That's what I'm looking into."

Andrea declined, asking for more time to consider if she had any options. Her cynicism still dominated her attitude. She had spent the last year looking for a career and was burnt out on the subject.

That left me at the end of the line to give my perspective. Preoccupied as I was with my building, I hadn't thought much about it. "Space. Not outer space, but working space, that's what I want to work on. If you're right Sam, then there's a real need for flex space for small and growing companies. We don't need huge sprawling industrial buildings here, but the right kind of operating space is critical. At my age and stage that's where I want to invest both my time and my money."

Sam seemed pleased with the answers.

"Not bad, not bad at all for our first go around on possibilities. Most of you have some idea of what you might do. Happy hour is on the horizon, so I want you to put more thought into this overnight and I want to leave you with one other idea. It's not an industry, but a growing source of opportunity. As Jake pointed out retirement is the basis for many changing needs, and, therefore, opportunities. But retirement itself is a new challenge for hundreds of thousands of business owners in North America. Business succession offers a wealth of opportunities.

Many of these business owners need to sell their business to fund their retirement. A lot of them are niche businesses with a future. As Martin said, startups are critical for future growth, but survivorships offer proven opportunity for new, younger owners. How might some of you capitalize on this predictable trend? Think about it.

"So on to happy hour. Today's guest is David Saxon. David started his business three years ago and he just turned eighteen. No alcoholic drink for him either, Dominic. I noticed that he arrived a few minutes ago, so take a quick five minute break to fill your glass and then we'll resume and David can share some experiences with you."

There was a rush to the bar highlighted by a level of enthusiasm reflected in the buzz of conversation. In just the second day allegiances were developing and age was not a factor. Youth was moving toward welcoming the perspective of age. Maturity could feel the charge associated with a transfusion of the passion of innocence. As they merged, the sum of the parts were showing early signs of outperforming the individual components. Sam was all smiles.

CHAPTER FOURTEEN

The Exuberance of Youth

David was at least six foot five and towered over all of us. Like Dominic he had just graduated from secondary school, but he wasn't a local. It turned out that he lived near Sam, who had become one of his first customers. He had driven out of the city that day out of loyalty.

Sam's introduction was short and enthusiastic, but David's talk was revealing. As commanding as his appearance might be, David was a shy, unassuming teenager who just happened to find an idea that left him with twenty-five thousand dollars in the bank as he tried to decide what to do next. University, or skip it? As Sam wrapped up his introduction you could see David tense up, and initially he spoke faster than normal.

"Okay, so making my own company all started when I was fifteen looking for a part-time job. I was handing out tons of résumés but wasn't getting anywhere. I was much smaller then and nobody wanted to hire a fifteen-year-old. I was frustrated until my dad told me about this Ontario government program called Summer Company. To qualify you have to be between fifteen and twenty-nine and you can't be working more than twelve hours at another job. You can start almost any type of business as long as it's independent. You don't have to register as a corporation and if you are accepted you receive a grant of three thousand dollars to start the business. When I heard about the three thousand dollars I wanted to do it. It seemed like a lot of money at the time; probably not so much if you were twenty-nine. So I decided to apply. The application consisted of a business plan and cash flow chart. With a little help from my parents I could do that. I knew how to work with Microsoft Excel from school and they helped me with the assumptions. We did three different scenarios because I had to do a lot of guess work and I really wasn't sure how it would go. I ended up getting accepted, and I was the youngest person in the program. It provided me with a great experience and the satisfaction of being my own boss at fifteen. I really liked that part. Starting a company at fifteen is great. It seemed easy, maybe a little too easy.

"I call my company Juniors for Seniors. The idea started with my next-door neighbour who was older and needed help for raking leaves, shovelling snow, and computer training. Looking back at my three years of running my own business I can't think of any job I'd rather have taken. This was the best job I could possibly have had while in school. It was flexible and could work around my schooling and sports, plus I was making and learning way more than anyone stuck at McDonalds or some other retail job.

"As you can tell from the name, I tailored my company toward seniors. Most of my business came from widows who wanted to continue living in their house but couldn't keep up with all the upkeep. Word of mouth was the only advertising I needed. I could have made the business much bigger but I didn't want employees. Maybe I could have made more money but I enjoyed the flexibility and the money was good enough. I used the grant to buy some basic equipment, but found most of my customers had their own. They really seemed to trust me. Something I found interesting was that a lot of the time the widows just wanted to talk. I guess they were lonely. The funny thing is I would go over to work on a specific thing that maybe should take an hour and I would spend an hour eating fresh baked goods, like lemon squares or banana bread, while talking about what was going on with their grandkids and then finally I would go to work for what seemed to be like ten minutes after all of this. Sometimes I felt guilty, but my customers seemed happy, especially when I helped them with their new computers or their cellphones. All my older customers can text and that's how they contact me now. It's been interesting hearing about people's lives, working hard on the specific jobs given to me, and most of all eating! What a great combination for a guy my age!

"Another game I came up with was trying to make the best out of my business by adding small goals for each visit so I didn't get bored. For example, I worked for one lady who was so nice it became kind of annoying. So I challenged myself to get her to say a specific word. The word I chose before I went to work one day was 'pickle,' so the whole day while working with her I was doing everything I could think of to get her to say pickle. About ten minutes before I left I finally tricked her into saying it. The story has nothing to do with my business, but it met a need for me — it made the time go by quicker and it made my work time fun.

"When you own your own company you have no choice but to learn important skills like problem solving and time management. Over my three years of cutting grass I have come to recognize the small things that made me productive, like how to cut grass the quickest or in a way that makes a specific yard look the nicest. Then you have to find the median method, where the lawn looks the nicest in the least amount of time. Now I know I could teach others if I decide to continue and choose to take on employees and expand.

"Experience is a great teacher. One customer decided to cut some small trees down in her backyard. I assumed that she would have it cut all the way down to the ground, so I didn't check before cutting the lawn. However, when I ran over the area with the lawn mower it actually bent my blade ninety degrees down. This happened the last night in the summer before I was supposed to go away. On top of that I still had another lawn to cut before dark.

The good thing was that from previous experiences I always knew to carry a vice grip in my van when cutting grass so I was able to fix the problem and get back to work before dark. Being prepared helps solve problems and it saves time and frustration.

"I suppose that the biggest thing I learned about being your own boss is that you have to be passionate and really love what you're doing. Otherwise you're not going to succeed. You have to go above and beyond and put in 110 percent because no one else will do it for you, but it's worth it. I'm not sure if that helps anyone here, but if you're interested in having your own business, I really recommend that you try it."

There was enthusiastic applause for David. The kid had made all of us smile through his innocence. It was like catching Donovan at the beginning of what he had built. David was younger, more innocent, less glib, but insightful all the same and more charming in a less sophisticated way than the dapper smooth talker that Donovan had become. David was a smart, energetic kid to whom all of us could relate. I could almost taste that freshly baked banana bread. He was one of us "ordinary people," but by fifteen he had already run the gauntlet of starting a business. More reason to be excited.

CHAPTER FIFTEEN

Putting the Pedal to the Metal

It was already the third day out of six. Our time was flying by and I was no further ahead on the development of my building. I really liked what I was hearing and appreciated the associations that were developing, but what good would they be? I was tempted to break Sam's rule and bring it up at the house but elected not to, at least not yet.

As usual Sam and I were the last to arrive the next afternoon. Everyone else was in their seats engaged in conversations, basically networking and exchanging ideas. Maybe that's what I was missing by spending so much time with Sam. I'd ask him what he thought after today's session. As usual Sam started right in.

"Let me premise this by saying that our speaker last night is an exceptional young man; polite, well-spoken, plus diligent and hard working. I can say that because he worked for me, although it appears I might owe him some baked goods to keep up with his other clients. But for a few minutes forget his age and analyze what you can take away from his talk. So what did you think about David?"

Andrea was all smiles, "I thought he was very cute." Her comment brought catcalls from her brother and Jake. She quickly backpedalled, "Not like that, you idiots. I mean the way he talked about his business had a sense of innocence and naïveté about it. After all he started when he was fifteen, just an average guy needing a job, pretty much the same story as Donovan and most of us. His goals were less lofty because he's a high school student with different needs. He wasn't as dynamic as Donovan, but I think he offered some good insights."

I thought so too, and since I wanted to become more active in the group I said so.

"It seemed to me that he'd learned several of the most basic ideas of being an entrepreneur, such as the need for going above and beyond, giving your customers what they want, keeping the focus on your personal goals so you don't let the business take over your life, the importance of solving problems and being prepared for them, the need to do more than one set of projections as a framework, and the possibility of growing the business if he elects to do that instead of going to school. Sam, you once told me that just because you can do something it doesn't mean that you should. I think David knows that and is considering all his options fully. He may not have the business savvy that Donovan has developed, but he showed me plenty of common sense in his approach and appreciation of his business. He definitely has pride of ownership and that's great to see in a person his age."

For once Martin and I agreed on something.

"He surprised me," said Martin. "I agree with Nick. He wasn't sophisticated in any sense of the word and if you asked him specifically about business concepts, I doubt he could answer. However, in the process of informally describing his experience running his one-man show, with no mentoring other than the possible exception of his parents, he managed to define some very important principles that are universal. If you dissect what he said it's fairly impressive."

The comments from Doris and Margaret were along the same lines. Dominic was confident that given the same opportunity he could have done as much or more than David had accomplished.

That reflected a little bit of teenage macho competitiveness, but it was good to see a more confident Dominic back in the fray. Paul was more glowing.

"I'm really getting excited about your mentoring idea. I think I could help David become a terrific success. With my experience and contacts and his common sense business approach we could do interesting things. I did sense that he might not have the drive to build a scalable business, but that could still develop. That was the one negative I got out of his comments."

"Paul gives him more credit than I would," Hannah said. "Donovan was not that much older and he very quickly saw the upside and possibilities to grow his business. David does not. The market appeal of a name like Juniors for Seniors is every bit as appealing as Student Decorators. Frankly, I thought that David fell short on the very task you were pushing us on yesterday. He failed to see the real opportunity."

"I kind of agree with Hannah," Jake said. "David is a nice kid and he has learned a lot, just as Nick and Martin suggested. But at this point he is not fully mature. He doesn't see the opportunity because he doesn't need to see it. The problem for him was the summer job. He solved that for his high school years. If he does go to university his needs will change and he'll benefit from his experience. He loved being his own boss. I bet he'll grow that business then because he will need more from it."

Sam was pleased and he said so.

"That's impressive. Quite a few differing conclusions about the results and possibilities over what a eighteen-year-old has accomplished. I'm particularly pleased with the comments made by Hannah and Jake. For sure David has learned some important fundamentals. He can do this again and I think he will. But the point I wanted to make is that he doesn't see the opportunity yet. Maybe you wouldn't either if you hadn't heard Donovan first. That's why I changed the order. Originally David was to speak Monday and Donovan yesterday. I think that order would have given you a more favourable opinion of David, which he deserves. I am going to introduce David to Donovan and see if that exposure changes his approach. All of which brings us back to today, to see how we can identify opportunities for all of you.

"Before we finish today I'm going to divide you into groups based on how I see your abilities and interests. Over the next three days I want each of those groups to present a business concept that you feel can be converted into a viable venture. We're going to discuss the pros and cons of each proposal and try to refine it right here. By Saturday night I expect every one of you to be in the earliest stage of a viable startup venture. So to be clear, each group will brainstorm and present their initial ideas tomorrow, and we'll refine them all day by day.

"But before we divide up I want to discuss the business succession issue I mentioned yesterday. I look at this situation as a vast pool of opportunities, one that is a critical part of our economy. Many of these are niche businesses and important local job creators. They are not multi-nationals. They may well be active in the global economy, but their interests lie right here at home, not chasing profits around the world. The owners have worked hard for years on the assumption that their business will fund their retirement. Many of them dreamed of their operations becoming second- or even third-generation businesses. That's not happening on a large scale because the second generation often isn't interested for a whole range of reasons. There is a huge opportunity for young people to cultivate these companies and become engaged, secure valuable mentorship, and eventually buy them up through an earn-out arrangement, which is a win-win situation. The original owner waits a little longer for his money but secures substantially more than a quick sale will yield. The new owner acquires a viable business primarily through sweat equity. With so many businesses coming up for sale it will be a buyer's market, with large companies driving hard bargains. Sellers will be looking for better options. Another potential area of synergy lays in applying tech and tech solutions to a whole slew of these niche companies that are lagging behind on the technology factor. The upside of this is the potential for the new owners to improve the productivity and the product offerings coming out of these businesses.

"I'm not sure how to tap into this huge potential, but I hope that maybe one idea reflected in your proposals. The concept is not new. Family-owned businesses have been transferred from generation to generation in informal, effective earn-out arrangements forever. As you know, that's exactly the plan Nick was pursuing. The real issue here is to identify industries and specific businesses that can endure in this fast-paced global world. Are there any questions up to this point?"

I had some different thoughts since I had been sabotaged by the sale of a family business to a third party, in my case a U.S. competitor who wanted to secure market share. I was sceptical and I thought that expediency would lead most retiring owners to a quick sale.

"Sam, don't you really think that most of these companies are going to be sucked up by large corporations who have been hoarding cash and are looking for growth from acquisition?"

"Not necessarily, Nick, not with the volume of sales that are expected. If that's the way this plays out there will be a glut of companies coming on to the market. As I just said, it will likely create a buyer's market, which will mean much lower prices for the sellers. Sale to a friendly buyer by a mentoring seller will keep businesses off the market, secure a better selling price, and avoid the outright closure of more companies. If the buyers are primarily large companies they will be after market share and you'll see more individual companies closed, less products and services being produced in North America, and increasing rates of localized structural employment like we've seen on a large scale in Detroit."

The whole group was paying attention now. Doris asked the next question.

"How do you see this matching process taking place? I mean, you have a huge pool of potential sellers and an equally large pool of potential buyers, provided they know and understand the prospects, but it's without a system to broker deals. It seems like a logistical nightmare to me."

Sam laughed out loud. "Sorry, Doris, but you did just describe the fundamental nature of how the real estate market works — large pools of buyers and sellers that intersect resulting in a sale. Maybe one of your ventures will come up with a solution to bring them together."

Doris didn't back down.

"That's an analogy, Sam, but maybe not a good one. There are large networks of real estate firms with well-defined communications systems that bring buyers and sellers together. You don't get to live in a house for five years and learn about it from the seller before you start the process of buying it. Individual houses have much more in common than private businesses. Due diligence is much more complicated. Good will is a factor that doesn't exist in real estate. This is a much more complicated problem, even if it is an opportunity."

Now Sam wasn't laughing. "You may be right about the analogy, but remember the mindset of an entrepreneur. We're talking about 'how,' not 'if' this is going to happen. You just gave me an example of prison thinking: reasons why this opportunity can't be capitalized on. We need to get the word 'can't' out of your vocabulary. I'm hoping that one of your groups may come up with some viable ideas. On the other hand this may be an area where none of you are interested. We'll see about that. In the meantime there are two specific interests within our overall group that I want to address. Two of you came here with specific ideas that you wanted to pursue. Margaret wanted to become a social entrepreneur.

"I've been struggling to find some ideas for her, starting with a good example of social entrepreneurship on a local level. The determining premise is applying innovative solutions to social problems. Proponents focus on attacking societal problems that governments either can't or won't tackle. Success revolves around achieving positive change for the greater common good. Usually the mechanism is a group or an organization that collectively takes on a serious problem for society. Of course there are a host of opportunities that can start on a local level. Individual initiative is a powerful force. A retired mayor has a great platform, but it *is* a local one. Regardless, almost every meaningful organization starts with a single powerful voice who becomes an excellent recruiter based on a cause that others can embrace. Margaret has the voice and the ability to recruit. We need to find her a cause. So we need some help from you, people who live in this community. What are some of the issues that need attention?"

Doris was active in a number of local charities, all of which could use more help.

"Margaret, we could really use your help at the food bank. A public person like you could increase what we raise three or four times over what we collect now."

There was an awkward hesitation before anyone else spoke. Finally I felt that I had to speak.

"That's a great idea, Doris, and it would work, but I think Margaret wants to start something new. The food bank is well established and the organization is in place."

Martin tried to help clarify things as well.

"Since I read Sam's book I've been looking into this concept of social entrepreneurship. As far as I'm concerned it sounded like an oxymoron. It doesn't seem right to include those two words in the same sentence. But as Sam pointed out, free enterprise is just one environment in which entrepreneurs flourish. I see that now. Charity is great and it brings relief to a multitude of needy people, but it doesn't solve problems. Charity makes life bearable, but it doesn't produce opportunity. Homeless people will stay homeless unless we address the problems that got them there. Feeding helps.

Providing a bed helps. But the underlying problem remains until we get to the root of it and diffuse it. As I understand it, that's the real potential of social entrepreneurship: to apply entrepreneurial principles to social issues and find enduring solutions."

Hannah wanted to encourage her grandmother. I think she realized that Margaret liked the notion of being entrepreneurial in a public way but didn't really understand how to go about it. Sam recognized the same lack of understanding, which is why he had initiated the discussion.

"Maybe you should be looking at newer problems Grandma," Hannah said. "You know, developing issues that either aren't recognized or haven't been solved. Sam keeps hammering us that there are many evolving issues in today's world that are broad-based but suppressed and ignored, sometimes because pointing them out is politically incorrect. You know, things like youth unemployment, racial profiling, drugs in schools, expanding poverty, the cost of education, localized structural unemployment, elder services, and elder care, to name a few. Too many of these are just being accepted as the new norm. I'm pretty sure as mayor you know more about some of these issues than most of us. I think your best bet is to choose an important concern and get out ahead of it. Pick one or two and we can discuss them here. Is that all right Sam?"

However, it was Margaret, not Sam, who answered her granddaughter. "Thanks, dear. And I thought I would be mentoring you and giving you the benefit of my experience. That's fine with me. I have a lot to consider, and you're right, many of these problems do make it to the mayor's desk and not enough are leaving there with a solution. Let me think about this on my own tonight."

Now it was Sam's turn. "Thanks Hannah, Martin, Nick, and Doris for your suggestions and comments. Nick my second concern is you. All you really wanted from me when we started were suggestions on how to fill up your building. I want you to move beyond that and look at the building as a resource. You've heard me say it enough — entrepreneurs are the catalyst that put all other resources to work. You have a resource: operating space with few limitations. I want you to expand your thought process and stop thinking of the vacant space as a problem and start looking at it as an opportunity. Over the next three days you're going to hear a lot of ideas for new ventures. Keep your mind open. Some of those ventures may offer you opportunity or you may be able to offer them one. Your problem is not finding tenants, it's putting the space you have to work in the most productive way.

"Time is almost up. These are the groupings that I want to work together to develop proposals for new ventures: Nick and Andrea, Martin and Dominic, Paul and Hannah, Doris and Jake, and since we have an extra senior, Margaret will work with me. These groups are not carved in stone. I fully expect that as ideas shift people will seek different alliances as well. There needn't be just two people in one venture. That's up to you, and you can bring in others depending on how many viable ventures we come up with. But this all starts by you coming tomorrow prepared to put ideas forward.

"Now it's time for happy hour. Today's speaker is George Picard. We'll start with George in about five minutes."

CHAPTER SIXTEEN

The Teenage Mentor

Sam told us very little about our speaker in his brief introduction. That's because there was an interesting twist to his story, best explained directly by George, who turned out to be the mirror image of David Saxon, literally. His business was two years old, operating under the name Sunshine for Seniors — sound familiar? David Saxon started his business three years ago, and his mother's maiden name was Picard. That's right — George had been pushed into an early retirement and found a mentor in his grandson, a fact which he was eager to share.

"I am very proud of what David has accomplished. When I got the golden handshake I needed to work. I wasn't ready to sit around all day, and frankly I needed some money to supplement my pensions. Like David I started by myself, providing a whole range of services for seniors, inspired by what he'd done that first summer, but doing things quite different than yard work. I started by driving seniors to appointments, taking them grocery shopping, to the drugstore, to their grandchildren's sporting events, to restaurants, to the theatre, to the airport, to church, to synagogue, even to funerals — wherever they wanted to go. Then I expanded by doing the grocery shopping for those who needed it. Before long I was picking out birthday cards, anniversary cards, and sympathy cards. Then I helped write them. I took photos and emailed them to family members. Soon I was doing birthday, Christmas, even Hanukkah shopping. Then I had another idea and I started locating services for clients and rating them based on experience. If you needed an electrician, a plumber, or a painter I could bring one in, expedite the quote, and make sure the work was done on time. I liked building relationships and sourcing all kinds of products and services. For all of this I charge out my time at twenty-five dollars an hour plus gas. People were more than willing to pay it. Like David I get almost all my customers by word of mouth. Before long I had to hire more drivers. I now have eight others working for me.

"The inspiration for the company name came from a comment made by one of my first clients, a ninety-one-year-old lady who had been housebound. One day as I arrived to pick her up, she said 'George, you're like a ray of sunshine every time you arrive. It gives me a lift every time you give me a lift.' That's become our motto: 'Get a lift from getting a lift.' I only hire cheery people. Every driver gets a joke book with three thousand old jokes in it and we use them to make our clients laugh. It's always a better day when you laugh. David probably told you that many of these people have little outside contact and often they want to talk. More than that, they need to talk. I knew that from David but I also know it myself, seniors like to have young people around. However, they also like to be around other seniors who are healthy, happy, and active. We set an example.

"I guess we're not really entrepreneurs. All my people are very focused on balance. They don't need as much as young people. The money's a supplementary income for all of them. Of course we also get tips, even though we discourage them. The work is rewarding. It doesn't feel like work and we make friends. That's another thing we do; we bring friendship to people who have lost most of their friends and it revitalizes many of them. We sort of reintegrate them to society. All kinds of different people recommend our services: doctors, lawyers, grocers, restaurants, and more. We arrange a lot of early bird dining with restaurants, bringing in seniors around 4:30 for special rate, lower volume meals. The restaurants like it and the customers are happy getting in and out before the noisy younger diners arrive. Often they don't even see each other. Now I've bought a little mini bus and we're starting to do day trips. Not large bus trips that last all day, just more intimate groups of about six, less hustle and bustle. Most of them are half days, so not great distances since our clients do get tired.

"All through this David has been my mentor. He actually got me my first two clients who he'd worked for the previous summer. Ironic, isn't it? We all want to insulate and protect our children and our grandchildren. They're not supposed to solve our problems. And who would think that I would have my own business after forty plus years working in an auto parts factory? And then to have my grandson give me the idea, that's just over the top. I'm not sure what David is going to do. I want him to keep going to school because I know it will increase his opportunities, but I'm pretty confident he'll be fine.

"I understand that most of you older folks are like me, needing something but not sure where to find it. My advice is simple: don't over complicate it. What we do is very basic. We solve simple bread and butter problems for older people who can't solve them for themselves anymore. There are a millions ways to find situations like this. If you understand life, you can create opportunity. Thanks very much for inviting me today."

George received a few questions from the group after finishing and he talked directly to most of us, certainly all of the senior group. He and Martin had something in common, having both worked in the auto parts sector. Jake spent a lot of time with George and had a lot of questions for him. They stayed engaged in conversation well after every one else was diverted.

The rest of us, who had been paired off by Sam, were distracted and each of us ended the afternoon in some form of animated conversation with their newly designated partner speculating on ideas to present the next day. There was a sense of urgency to produce something worthwhile. Running out of time, Paul suggested that we take advantage of the room and meet at 1:30 before the session so we would have more time to prepare. While we all agreed to meet early the next day, there was a prevailing sense of competiveness in the discussions and a reluctance to share progress with other groups. Whether it was fear of failure or determination to win, we all intended to impress Sam.

CHAPTER SEVENTEEN

Putting Meat on the Bone

All of us showed up promptly at 1:30. While there was a sense of purpose pervading the room, I could also feel a cloak of doubt encompassing it. There was a will to create, but something was lacking, at least for me. Sam had paired me with Andrea. Initially she had no ideas reflecting her high level of cynicism, and my focus was the building and nothing else. That made us too narrow and almost devoid of ideas. Having Sam at my house was no help at all. He wouldn't discuss possibilities with me even after I heard him talking to Margaret on the phone that morning. Beyond that he was a distraction. The night before we had watched my two grandsons play football and that's all he wanted to talk about.

I arrived at the meeting disappointed in myself. Owning the building was stifling my innovation. But Andrea offered a good suggestion.

"Nick, I think your building is great for you, but I don't see any opportunity for me related to it, at least not yet. Maybe I should transfer to a different group. What you might do is consider some of the other ideas that come out today and look for tenants out of these new ventures. Does that make any sense? I'm going to do the same with a different purpose — searching for a role. Maybe you can offer a home to one of the ventures and maybe one of the ventures can become a home for me. Remember what George said last night: keep it simple."

That became our strategy for that first day of reporting back to Sam.

Right after we agreed on this, Martin came over to speak to me. Just as Sam walked in the door Martin said, "Nick, I know that Sam has had a varied career but did he ever start anything later in life himself?"

For the briefest moment I was embarrassed. There was no doubt that Sam had heard. The implication was "Does Sam know what he's talking about?" At least that's how I took it.

Sam didn't, and called Martin out.

"That's fair game, Martin. So let's discuss it. At sixty-five I decided to become an author. Not for the money; I wanted to validate my career and help others. It seemed like a straightforward goal — not easy, but well defined. All of us have a book inside, just screaming to get out. Of course we do. I knew that when I started. It couldn't be that difficult. Two years later, after hours spent staring at a blank page followed by extended sessions of relentless padding to get the word count up, numerous plot changes, and the creation of characters that came out of nowhere, I had it — that first book, in my case a novel. Five hundred and ten pages of insightful dialogue, my own creation. All my friends and family loved it. The most difficult part was behind me. Getting published was inevitable, a slam dunk.

"Not quite. Writing a book proved to be the easy part followed by the next eighteen months spent enduring the dichotomy of never-ending evaluations combined with constantly hearing the lecture regarding the need for *shameless self-promotion*. The prevailing wisdom was and is that an author must have a website, a blog, and prepare an endless stream of submissions and query letters, almost all of which will never be acknowledged. This masochistic practice of silent appraisal without feedback leads to the inevitable conclusion that you have to self-publish, but under no circumstances use a 'vanity' publisher, because that will seal your fate as a hopeless amateur. At this point confusion rules the day. You have no opinion that is remotely close to being objective, alternating between the fear that what you have produced is rubbish and the daydream of accepting the academy award for best original screenplay. Quiet evenings spent fanaticizing with your spouse about which of your favourite actors can play the key roles in your story. Weekends searching out potential publishers and agents, attending 'how-to' seminars on getting published, inevitably emphasizing that you are really on your own in a context totally unfamiliar, highlighting the adjective 'self' in that recurring, persistent theme of *shameless self-promotion*. This is not who I am, so reinventing myself one more time was inevitable, and that's an ongoing process.

"Perhaps my favourite low point was an hour long presentation by one of Canada's most successful literary agents. She was quite blunt setting out the rules including: 'Don't ever send me anything other than an email query letter. I get at least seventy-five inquires a day, all by email. If I don't like what I read in the first two lines I simply hit delete.' Then, for emphasis, she stated with obvious pride: 'Incidentally, I would have rejected *The Da Vinci Code*.' Now that's encouragement. I still send her regular emails if for no other reason to keep her count up. My most brilliant prose, my most humourous anecdote, my most insightful analysis, and my most heartfelt criticism of her methods, all met the same fate she would have dealt Dan Brown — Delete! Delete! Delete!

"Did you know that in this age of computerization there are far more books being generated than ever before? With total logic, in the face of this new flood of creativity, publishers have abandoned any attempt to assess unsolicited manuscripts. No longer are junior staffers assigned to look at unknowns. This is left to the few reputable literary agents in Canada, and we all know how well that is working out.

"So I went back to the drawing board. It was time to turn to the world of freelance professionals and get a frank assessment of the product. First stop was an evaluation by a professional editor with a six-hundred-dollar price tag, premised by the statement '75 percent of what I evaluate is garbage.' Now waiting for that was tough. No one wants to be classified as 'garbage,' even if almost everyone else is. I passed that one somehow. By the way, did I mention that the conventional wisdom is that a first novel should be between 80,000 and 100,000 words and 350 pages, not 160,000 words and 510 pages like mine? Remember all those nights padding the word count? Time to take those babies back out. Remember all those brilliant explanations included to save your dimwitted readers from making incorrect assumptions — they have to go. More advice: 'You must let the reader discover in their own way, and for God's sake pick up the pace.' My characters didn't suck. My plot was kind of interesting. My freelance editor became my link to the industry, my literary personal trainer, part drill instructor, part sister confessor, she kicked and coddled me down the road to self-respect as an author and gave me the will to put myself out there.

"Now I was freshly inspired. My work was not garbage. With a just little bit more effort, I might have something. Five rewrites and numerous more query letters later. After rewriting the book five times I began to hate it with newfound passion. Not really, but it's somewhat like the way you feel about your first born after three days of the runs and fifty diaper changes. You still love them but the poop has got to stop. Does this sound like an exercise in entrepreneurship? Throughout all of this I kept trying to find a way to make it happen, to become a published author.

"Then I made a breakthrough. I met a publisher who was interested. The end was in sight. Not really. They liked my book but really preferred to publish non-fiction. Why didn't I write about my career? When I did that they really liked the book, but could I write a series? Could I get some high profile endorsements? Could I? Could I? Could I...?

"Being an author is a creative process, not just creating the book but creating the real product. In my case, Sam the author. You have to be a producer, a publicist, a public speaker, and fill every other role required to manage the business of your book. Should it be any different? Can anyone else do it quite the same way? On top of that, for me writing my book brought out an element of social entre-preneurship. Just what we're doing here, mentoring people about a trend that I think is critical for society. My career is relevant. My experience is helpful. So that's me and retirement. None of this was likely if I wasn't entrepreneurial. I would have given up long ago. So that's the long answer to your question Martin. Are you satisfied?"

It was totally unexpected, but his rant about his experience with the publishing industry was a solid reminder that our mentor had been there and done that. Martin looked a little shell-shocked but he was smiling. "Can't add much to that Sam, but if there were any doubts they're gone."

"That felt good," said Sam, "the mental equivalent to a brisk morning run before work. My head is clear now, but today is not about me. It's time to hear your first drafts. What has your brain-storming produced? Martin, it seems only fair play that we start with you and Dominic."

I thought Martin might be flustered by Sam's reaction, but he was totally calm as he stood to present his and Dominic's initial conclusions.

"Let me remind you how the two of us started. When Sam asked us where we saw potential the other day, I suggested that I wanted to work with startups and Dominic saw opportunity in providing some form of service. On the surface that seems to be far apart, but I'm open to all startup ideas of any type in any area. Actually, after listening to Sam I'm far less preoccupied with tech startups. We've heard from three speakers, all of whom found ways to fill an existing need in a different way that distinguishes them. I like that. I'm from the traditional economy and comfort-able looking for opportunities there. Dominic is interested in the service industry, but he's open to others. Like most kids his age he's a bit of a gadget geek, so we're looking for areas where we can apply technology rather than develop it. I will never understand today's technology, but I do know that we've only scratched the surface of applying it. Both of us think we need to recruit more members to our team, either from other groups here or outsiders. So that's where we stand right now. We're focused on working with startups but still figuring out how. We need more time, and we'll give you an update tomorrow. At least, if that's your plan Sam?"

Sam was shaking his head.

"It's a start, but barely. You're going to have to do a lot better than that by tomorrow. Stop dealing in generalities. So far there's nothing remotely close to a business concept that I can see. Let's hear from Doris and Jake next. I hope that you're thinking in terms of a specific business concept."

I could tell they weren't. Were any of us that far? I doubted it. Jake decided to face the issue straight on.

"We're not, Sam. I want to focus on elder care, just as I said the other day. Doris has spent her entire career in real estate and she feels that her experience is best served as a property manager. We simply have different interests, so we talked about it a lot and now we agree, so if you don't mind I'd like to trade Doris, with her blessing, to Nick's team in exchange for Andrea. Doris and I both feel that she can help Nick. From what Dominic has told me, Andrea did a work term in high school with a physiotherapist and has always had some interest in health care. Andrea, would you be willing to work with me to see what we can come up with?"

It made sense. Doris could definitely help me. She'd had good exposure to commercial leasing. Her interest in property management surprised me, but it was good news. Andrea didn't hesitate.

"I'd like to make the change. I don't see any role for me with Nick's project, but Doris is a good fit. I am interested in health care and I agree with Jake. It's a growth area for sure and should be stable. Let's do it!"

That was the most enthusiasm that Andrea had shown all week. Her rejection of me actually felt good since we weren't a good fit. The only downside was that the four of us had reverted to our peer groups. Sam ignored that. On the other hand he had encouraged us to make changes.

"Well, Nick, I expect your report is going to be fairly short now."

"Short and sweet," I agreed. "I like Jake's suggestion. I've known Doris most of my life and can't believe I didn't think of it myself. She has the perfect experience, so that's positive. Andrea did make a great suggestion. I want all of you to know that on her recommendation I am watching and assessing the ventures you develop as potential tenants. So as your ideas evolve, keep that in mind and talk to me to see if we can work together. That's my focus right now, but Doris may have other ideas."

"Good!" Sam bellowed, louder than he planned. "That's what I'm looking for! Cross pollination of business concepts. All of you should be looking for ways to develop in concert. This is a small- to medium-sized market. Alliances are critical, and it goes far beyond location. Complimentary businesses are possible and they can reinforce each other. There is no ecosystem here that meets your needs so you need to create one. Keep that in mind. I know you've been protective about your ideas. I could see it last night when you all went to separate corners of the room. Almost all of you kept looking over your shoulder to see or hear what the others were doing. That's fine when you're in direct competition, but you're not. Forget about pleasing me. I'll be gone next week. Share ideas and explore ways to work together. Who knows, we might only end up with two ventures and still keep everyone involved. Now Paul and Hannah, what have you come up with?"

I was surprised to see Paul defer to Hannah, but she didn't disappoint him.

"As you know Paul is a well-respected accountant with many years of experience in industrial management. I am a postgraduate student working on my MBA, but I've been actively working in the startup community at the incubator at the university for the past three years. We want to build a financial advisory service that specializes in raising capital for non-tech startup companies. We especially want to build relationships with older and younger entrepreneurs who lack funding options. We have meetings with two banks and a venture capitalist tomorrow morning as well as the director of the university incubator. We are also researching some new, less regulated possibilities. We definitely want to work with potential startup ventures deriving from this program. All of you will need funding, so please sit down with Paul and I to discuss your needs as soon as possible. We will report back at tomorrow's session regarding our initial meetings. I think that covers everything. Do you have anything to add, Paul?"

"Just one thing. I feel the company that we're proposing highlights the benefits of the age association that Sam has been advocating. I have the experience and many contacts that can facilitate raising capital. Hannah is well tied into the startup culture and we hope to expand that with you into non-tech and duo-generational startups. Between the two of us we cover most of the bases. We also may want to add additional people. We will be insisting that our debtors develop an advisory board to mentor and foster sound decision making. If any of you are interested in serving on these boards please bring in your CV to review with Hannah and me."

Sam couldn't hide his pleasure at this presentation.

"I was hoping that you two would come through. I had a sense that you were likeminded and that your attributes and your interests were a good fit. That's excellent progress for the first day, after less than twenty-four hours of collaboration. I'm looking forward to your report tomorrow. So Margaret is next. She and I spoke on the phone last night, but I'm not sure where she stands today."

Margret had been a mayor for seven years and was used to the backing of a strong support team. She depended on municipal staff to research and recommend. With the exception of a rare situation that was politically sensitive where the impact on the electorate directed her away from a professional staff position, Margaret just accepted and ratified the staff recommendation. Now there were no staff to recommend, and for the first time in a long while she was on her own.

Margaret started in almost a whisper. "I'm still thinking of education. My initial goal is to find ways to restore parental involvement in the school system. Home and school associations were once a powerful educational tool. Both parents and teachers committed a lot of private time to facilitate social and cultural programs for students. This is a great challenge for me right here in this community, and if we do things right we can become a shining example of what can be accomplished in an environment where budgets are being slashed. I need to attract teachers and parents to rebuild this tradition and that's who I'll be recruiting. One last thing, I am committed to rebuild this organization and if I'm successful in my recruitment I'll have time for other projects. I'm interested in working in one of the ventures developed here if the opportunity arises."

Sam checked his watch. We had time to spare because none of these updates had taken very long. He needed to improvise and made a snap decision how he would.

"Speaking of education, there's a hot debate going on right now on the importance of post-secondary education. Dominic is wrestling with this decision right now. Is it worth the cost and the mounting debt? Is education delivering on opportunity? It's a debate that's very relevant to what we're doing here. We have two university graduates who are struggling to find their way, as well as two younger students who haven't committed to go on yet. I want to give our four youth entrepreneurs more to consider on this critical decision. We've reviewed some of these factors, but regardless here's my perspective on some of the pros and cons that new graduates from colleges and universities are facing.

"You just graduated and now you're educated. The world is your oyster, or is it? You know my opinion: the most important skill you can add today is the ability to create and manage your career. That's true with or without a post-secondary education. On the surface this is not the best time to graduate. There's a whole litany of reasons that you've already heard me mention. The cost of education is very high, bringing student debt to record levels.

Job stability is in decline. The distribution of wealth is skewed in favour of those at the top. Upward mobility is in jeopardy. The rate of change is increasing. All this means that your future is dependent on self-determination grounded in awareness of the world in which you live. In this environment you are your own brand and must plan on reinventing yourself throughout your work life. That means engaging in entrepreneurial thinking right at the outset of your career, starting with course selection. Whether you start a business, become a solopreneur, work in a large entity, or engage in social entrepreneurship, you have to become adaptable and resilient in a world dominated by change. Entrepreneurial thinking is about a mindset, not a skill set. Success is about finding a way, not knowing the way. In the era of Big Data this is essential. We will never know enough or understand enough of what we know. So abandon prison thinking and get started. With that in mind here are five ideas you need to reject and dismiss:

"One: Education guarantees you a future. Sorry, but you don't have it made: education never ceases and formal education just gives you more opportunities. There are no guarantees.

"Two: There are no jobs for graduates. There are barriers to entering the work force right today that are as insurmountable as we allow them to be. Resilience and adaptability start now.

"Three: Government will solve the employment problem. Would you really choose government as your advocate to solve any problem?

"Four: There is no future within small business. Life expectancy of all businesses is in decline. Strategic management of your career takes you where you can gain the most now! Small and flexible is a sound model for today's global world.

"Five: Millenials don't make good hires. Maybe you place a higher value on social media contact and demand access during the day but technology is your ally making you more productive than older generations.

"It's critical to shelve all of these misconceptions because invalid as they are, they add nothing to the debate. However, there are many reasons for confidence if you've just graduated. Here are ten for your data bank:

"One: Technology, your ally in learning, has lowered the cost of administration through the integration of many management tasks. A two-and-a-half pound laptop allows anyone to consolidate their accounting system, sales, marketing network, all communication, research, collections, and payments, not to mention a wide variety of personal needs into one portable notebook. Add in mobility via a smartphone and you are always accessible and connected. You have the potential to do it all, as a disruptor, within a large corporation or government agency or as an independent.

"Two: Big Data is generating new problems at record rates. Every problem is an opportunity. Education ultimately boils down to learning how to learn. Analytics will shorten the process, not replace it.

"Three: Social networking, another ally, has increased the reach of individuals, allowing market access on a much broader geographic scope. Services can be offered at great distance. Endorsements can be sought and received across the country or even worldwide. Credibility can be built quickly through performance. LinkedIn is a great tool to market your skills and pursue your career strategy. Education increases your reach and broadens your network.

"Four: Websites can be both affordable and first class, allowing an individual to build a professional image. Employee and entrepreneur alike can build their brand and market themselves. Content depends on substance.

"Five: Outsourcing is an established practice by which governments and large corporations are achieving flexibility, which rewards specialization right down to the individual level. Businesses may only want you part time, so find several of them and keep them happy. That process can start at graduation.

"Six: Acquisition is a principal way for large entities to find innovation-making startups, often founded on youth and enthusiasm — a great opportunity if you can join the right team. Small entrepreneurial firms offer a serious upside for recent graduates.

"Seven: Succession is a huge issue for hundreds and thousands of viable independent businesses in North America as the baby boom generation hits retirement, depending on their business, to fund their future. You can find a mentor that leads you to acquire your own business through an earn out that funds his or her retirement. Education shows commitment to a project that will appeal to potential sellers.

"Eight: Size is simply becoming a liability, so make good choices. There are many small viable market niches that large companies and foreign sourcing will never fill. Adaptability, resilience, and flexibility are essential in a world dominated by change. Align yourself with entrepreneurial thinkers.

"Nine: Opportunity is nowhere, opportunity is everywhere. It is the best of times, it is the worst of times. Recognizing opportunity is the cornerstone of success in every aspect of your career. Education opens doors, and in doing so, possibilities.

"Ten: Determination was the key to graduating. It is also the key to managing your career.

"I wanted to review these key factors to influence all of you as you strive to define viable new ventures that meet your needs. Many of them don't *require* education, but most *benefit* from it. Education and opportunity should be synonymous. You need to assess as much background information as possible before committing to any venture including education. If the solution to a successful career lies within your ability to create your own brand, the first step in that process starts with good strategic choices. Don't pursue a degree for the sake of status; education is a means to an end and has to lead to a path. In this era of Big Data education is and will always be, ongoing.

"I see it's time for happy hour, though it seems like no time at all since George was here. Today we have Brent Taylor from Tech Engagement. You may have heard of it. I've invited him because he's taken a different approach to building an incubator. I'm hoping that when you hear about the slant he's taken it might stimulate you to think outside of the box. Grab your drink of the day. We'll be starting in about ten minutes."

CHAPTER EIGHTEEN

A Mentoring Machine

As Sam was bolstering his introduction of Brent Taylor he managed to emphasize a few key factors that were relevant to us.

"Brent is the director of Tech Engagement, a successful incubator that has fostered the development of over fifty companies in this area. Most incubators are outgrowths of a university setting, located on or near university campuses, and are focused on nurturing the development of tech ventures, conceived by students or recent graduates, into scalable businesses. Brent decided to locate in Milton because of its central location, its rapid growth, its access to transportation, and its supply of lower-cost housing relative to the city proper. Instead of mentoring and nurturing students, he's chosen to focus on people in their early thirties with a tech background who've worked in the industry for at least five years. That's why he located in suburbia where many of them live.

"Like most incubators Tech Engagement provides space, a range of services, and mentoring. Instead of the 24/7 work pattern that characterizes tech startups run by students, peak time at Tech is between seven and twelve at night plus much longer hours on weekends. I've asked Brent to take a step back and comment whenever possible on how some of the methods and policies used at Tech Engagement might be modified or transferred from the tech world to the traditional economy. My personal goal is to expand the incubation system and approach far more into the mainstream of entrepreneurship that is lagging to some degree in the traditional economy. I'm very interested in Brent's observations on this. So nurse your drink, relax, and listen. I'm happy to give you Brent Taylor."

Brent was a serious academic type who no doubt revelled in the tech world. He was tall, thin, and wore dark glasses, a well-defined Buddy Holly look-alike for my generation, the typical tech geek for the younger one. I don't think he quite knew what to make of the audience. We were entirely too diverse for him. I was sure he didn't work with anyone under thirty or over forty. However, my impression of him changed once he started to speak and his passion began to show. In the flick of an eye, he transformed from a tech nerd into an animated speaker enthralled with his subject and a passionate promoter of entrepreneurs and new approaches to encourage them.

"Thanks for inviting me, Sam. Right out of the gate, there's definitely serious potential to move away from tech and duplicate some of the things that we're doing for ventures headed for the traditional economy. Incubation has many synonyms, including development, gestation, nurture, and evolution to name a few. We provide a protected environment that shields entrepreneurs when they're the most vulnerable — the startup phase. It's also the time in their careers when they most need mentoring. If entrepreneurship is going to fill the needs of the twenty-first century global economy we need more mentors. When you're encased in an incubator like ours, you develop powerful partnerships, support innovative initiatives, and explore business issues that need a solution. Our particular focus group brings everyday problems to the table — real problems for which active businesses need solutions. We're funded by business, not by the government. We do develop new companies, but we also foster change within larger companies that invest in us. Big business supports us because they have no choice. They have to change their culture and encourage what some are calling 'intrapreneurship.' Beyond that their main approach to growth is through acquisition. Most of our ventures start from employees working for large companies. These are people on the inside who see opportunity outside the organization, and are willing to provide sweat equity on their own time to take new products or services to market to prove viability. Because they are employees we are very conscious of protecting intellectual property. That's essential for preserving our relationship with the business community. Arguably many more products and ideas do mature through a combination of what an incubator provides in terms of support and a bootstrapping approach practiced by the founders that keeps the cost of development down. It's an efficient way to pursue both growth and opportunity. That's why the private sector supports us.

"Once the product or service is proven, large companies are potential buyers of these startups, with plenty of synergy to offer, mainly because of market penetration. We have proven that this is a cost-effective way to serve the needs of both individuals and large entities so that we cultivate as much money as possible from large multinationals. For individuals to succeed today they need to capture part of the increasing return that's going to capital. Wages are too limiting. Academics can be too immersed in the project and don't always get the economics. Our ventures come with experience and have a different perspective of the problems, the potential, and the market.

"Still, we're far from divorced from the university scene. Graduate students are insulated but their educators are well aware of the economic reality. A lot of our mentors and members of our advisory boards are professors from both the engineering and business faculties of several universities. It's a two-way street. Their involvement with us keeps them in touch with the business world in unique ways that carry over to their own incubators. Physically we're halfway between Kitchener-Waterloo and

Toronto. That's not a coincidence. We have five universities and as many colleges within fifty miles and good physical access to them. We believe it's time that competing groups in Southern Ontario accept that our area has the assets and diversity to create a major ecosystem. *But* it has to be a single co-operative and coordinated launch pad, not several competing ones, each with their own agenda. I don't see that happening yet, but on a small scale we achieve strong interaction from talented people from several universities bringing them together, if in a limited way. That mix of talent combined with gurus from the private sector allows us to provide world-class coaching and mentoring, access to capital, professional advice, and much more.

"So how does all of this apply to you and the mainstream economy? Did I mention that because of the way we're structured we are less pure tech development and more oriented toward the application of tech solutions? We're already part way between a tech incubator and what you can accomplish here. That's the engagement part of our name, and it means we're one step closer to the broader economy. You can take that last step. What I see as a possibility for you doing is building a different set of mentors. You're focus should be more general, focused on basic business issues, funding in particular, but all facets of business practice that it takes to run a business. We find that's a missing ingredient for most aspiring entrepreneurs, regardless of education. Even our seasoned founders need coaching on the fundamentals and that need is more pressing in the university-based incubator. Maybe it's a little less for us since most of our protégées have several years of business experience, but our ventures still lack many fundamentals. From what I understand you have a mixture here of rookies and veterans. That makes you different."

Brent seemed to have a grandiose sense of what we were about. What had Sam told him? Was Sam trying to forge something far beyond our expectations? No time to consider what, as Brent continued on.

"We view our incubator as a viable alternative to an MBA program. Most business schools rely heavily on well-motivated, experienced students coming back from the workforce to pay the freight and fill their post-grad classrooms. Sam was the first to convince me that our option is more appropriate for many because we're focused on producing successful entrepreneurs from people whose background has made them predisposed to become one but who may not have the resources for further education. It doesn't hurt that our founders continue in their jobs while their ventures mature. On average they're a little older with obligations. We're based securely on the foundation of motivation and determination cemented by sweat equity. As long as we have a stable of effective mentors our program works. Oh, I should mention that Sam is one of our mentors and sits on the advisory board for Tech Engagement."

Aha, a clue. Sam must be up to something beyond what I knew.

"Success for an incubator or accelerator is usually measured in terms of equity created. That success depends largely on building trust and support from investors. As Tech Engagement builds a track record of success we have more and more investors prepared to advance funds to our ventures as they mature and graduate from our program. We don't over commit. We can only handle a relatively small number of ventures in each session. There's definitely a different opportunity here, but If you choose to do something like this be selective and be demanding. Keep your ventures focused. Give them benchmarks. If they miss them kick them out. Don't let a culture of failure or procrastination develop. You don't need academics to the extent that we do. Build up a stable of mentors from the business world like we have. One of the criticisms of incubators is that they don't always build the right type of networking. That's another reason we moved away from the university environment and why we are financed by private companies as opposed to government. Never lose sight of the goals you have. If you do set benchmarks make sure they advance the company, not just achieve some meaningless goals that make your incubator look good.

"There is a feeling out there that we have too many competing parallel incubators. Some ventures manage to get engaged in more than one. Regardless, we don't have enough effective ones and most of the ones we do have focus strictly on tech innovations. Many of them concentrate on providing cheap space, sustaining bootstrapping and little else that's effective. Our goals go well beyond that, and yours should too. We're looking to create sustainable equity, not speculative equity that results from venture-capital-based accelerators. We're looking for a much higher success rate by producing hands-on management for a class of serial entrepreneurs who can and will do it again and again over their careers, and in the process invest locally more than internationally. We're not as enamoured with producing strictly scalable businesses. That's a process hoping to create more multinationals that join the club of the superrich: very prestigious, but few and far between. We have produced one of those and there may be more, but most of our ventures will turn into stable, viable companies who find stable niche markets and survive. We want to create businesses that create jobs. We're not satisfied with a one in ten success rate. In that sense we're second tier. In our wildest dreams we will never become Y Combinator, the gold standard of venture capital accelerators.

"As you know ideas and terminology from the tech world dominate the dialogue regarding entrepreneurs and entrepreneurship. I have come from that world, a fast and furious environment dominated by the need to get to market first, a world consumed with burn rate, high risk, and venture capital returns. The majority fail. There are few endeavours in the real world where a 10 percent success rate is considered acceptable, never mind good. North America was built on a dynamic productive manufacturing sector. A company producing 90 percent rejects would not survive. Unfortunately the tech industry is dominated by speculation, greed, and speed. The success stories are legendary. The failures on the scrap heap are deemed an essential part of the learning curve. We must learn from both type of results and build a better model. I'm afraid I've gone well over my time. Thanks very much for inviting me."

Wow! That was quite a different story than that of a eighteen-year-old boy, as impressive as David had been. I, for one, had a million and one thoughts firing around my head. I was excited. As I looked around the room everyone was beaming. Martin, Paul, Hannah, Dominic, Andrea, and Jake had already surrounded Brent, bursting with questions. Sam was standing back, enjoying the spectacle. As always there was method in his madness. I spent every night with him that week, never once allowed to talk about the sessions or his goals. Regardless, there had always been a plan and it was starting to emerge. There were two days left to achieve whatever goals he had set. How would they affect me? The whole process seemed so random. Had we picked people who were good enough to achieve something bigger and worthwhile, whatever that might prove to be? The million ideas were still whirling around in my head creating a sense of elation. I needed to digest some of them and put the real possibilities into perspective.

In the midst of all this commotion the session ended abruptly because it was just after five, Sam's hard and fast rule again. Despite a series of hastily arranged meetings between members of the various groups to make sense of it all, there was a state of confusion on how to proceed and prepare for the next day. Doris and I decided to talk on the phone that night and meet early the next afternoon if needed. The others were chattering on, unconstrained in their thought process with little or no sense of direction. I could hardly wait to see how things would change by the time we reconvened as a group and reality set in.

CHAPTER NINETEEN

Building Consensus

That night Doris and I spoke on the phone. It turned out that she was elated to be aligned with me in a field that she knew. Our hopes were high. I hadn't felt that positive since the day I'd found out my planned future had been sold out to a U.S. buyer. By the time we finished talking we'd made a decision on the position we would take with Sam.

Like the others we met early the next afternoon to consolidate our position. We were prepared to go it alone based on a combination of offering property management services and managing my rental property, or we were willing to be integrated into something grander if the other ventures proposed a comprehensive plan along the lines implied by Brent. If we went solo, Doris had a substantial amount of savings that might allow us to purchase a second building. In the interest of bootstrapping we decided we would prove our metal by filling up my building, relying on the expertise Doris had in renting commercial properties. Between the two of us we could manage that and hopefully some additional properties owned by others rather than paying for a professional property manager.

If something bigger emerged from the group discussion we agreed that we could have the benefit of built in demand that might develop to offer a serious opportunity for additional expansion. First we needed to know more. I was enamoured with the possibility of a mainstream economy incubator that could be housed in my building, but I wasn't at all sure that we had the resources or expertise to pull it off. I was also concerned that the revenue stream would be low and unreliable. That was the bigger picture that Doris and I had agreed on. We were prepared, even eager, to be part of developing the incubator on our own, provided Sam would participate. I presumed that was Sam's intention, but I was far from sure.

That was my mood and my take on the situation when our second-to-last session was about to start. Some of the other groups had had much longer meetings the night before and again that morning. All of them pressed me for information about Sam's plans. He was a big-picture guy and now that they knew there was one, they wanted information. Sam hadn't revealed even a crumb more to me and had spent the night talking to my wife while Doris and I were trying to figure things out by phone. Nothing changed when he arrived for our session. Continuing to be close-mouthed he didn't give anything else away as he started into the Friday discussions.

"That was quite a bomb Brent dropped on you last night. I didn't realize he could be so fiery. I half expected him to jump up at the end and shout 'so who's with me!' For a few minutes there his words were flowing so well he was the Patrick Henry of entrepreneurship, sort of 'give me opportunity or give me death!' I suppose that's a little melodramatic, but he was quite passionate and very suggestive. I liked most of what he said. You may suspect a lot of what he articulated flowed out of conversations that he and I have had, and if you do, you're right. Brent and I did explore some ambitious goals for this group the night before last, including some precedent-setting ideas that could provide a model for others. Regardless, that's for you to decide. What I need to know is how yesterday's presentation affected your thinking and influenced your concepts for ventures. Who wants to go first?"

Martin was on his feet and ready to speak. There was no other competition to go first. What he didn't realize was that all of the rest of us wanted to hear more before we spoke. One will seldom regret the things we don't say, but we are often haunted by what we do say. Sam's intentions weren't clear, so it seemed better to stay reserved and be prepared to go with the flow. Martin liked to shoot from the hip. That was one of the reservations I had about him. He wasn't much of a listener and liked the sound of his own voice, making him seem a touch superficial and even more self-centred.

"Our duo liked what we heard. If nothing else, Sam, you've given us hope and some great examples. I think Tech Engagement has wrestled with many issues that can be applied to the non-tech world. It's pretty heady stuff to go from where we are at the moment to the kind of comprehensive program that Brent was suggesting. We've bounced this around a lot last night. Dominic and I have two or three specific possibilities that we're considering. Our prime interest is working with startups, so we're big on the idea of starting an incubator for the real world as opposed to tech. An incubator would tie us into a wide range of startup opportunities and potential investments. With my management experience and Dominic's drive to recruit young people with unproven concepts we could make this work and find an active role with a range of interesting ventures. But if we're realistic we need a lot more depth and would have to recruit a whole range of mentors. I need more time to figure out the revenue stream. We may be able to do it, but we need help and adequate time, which could strain our resources. Regardless, that's one awesome project of serious interest for us.

"Next we've done a fair amount of investigation this week on the business succession issue that you described the other day. It's huge. We have a second proposal that could be a better fit for us related to that growing problem. We're assessing the notion of opening a business brokerage dedicated to matching up young talent with potential mentors who are looking for someone to take over existing businesses. My role would be to build contacts with owner-operated businesses with owners that are approaching retirement. Dominic's part would be to recruit young talent with the ability to learn and be mentored by the sellers that I contact. It's a matching process that revolves around structuring buyouts that work for both parties. We feel this is an area that lines up well with our collective strengths.

"That's not all. Our third proposed venture is to establish Dominic's servicing network. We plan to recruit seniors and juniors with a very broad range of skills, create a talent pool, and broker their services out, initially to seniors and professional couples who need reliable, timely help in a wide range of areas. We know there are many talented seniors who want or need to supplement their incomes. We don't think many of them want the responsibility of starting a full-scale business or even working full time. We can put seniors to work on a part-time basis and fill many specialized consumer needs, not just for seniors but for busy families with two working parents. For young people we will pair them up with a senior to learn different skills while they earn some money. The idea came from listening to David and his grandfather. We think that both groups would benefit from a company that takes care of the administration and marketing needs, allowing them to perform the work and mentor or be mentored without too many distractions. This would fundamentally be a booking exchange for services plus a teaching forum provided by seniors for youth.

"So right now we think we have three viable ideas, all of which we like. The major unknown is what the other groups hope to accomplish and what you're thinking, Sam. We're planning on burning some midnight oil tonight once we have a better sense of the landscape. I want to emphasize that we'll consider merging with another group if the possibility comes up today."

Impressive; there I was no other word for it. Martin and Dominic were serious and had sculpted out some great possibilities. Sam said nothing, but I could tell that things were falling into place for him. My only problem was that I wanted the incubator for my project. The more I thought about it the more it made sense for me and Donna to do it. All incubators were grounded in providing space. We could recruit mentors, Martin could even be one but we had the key ingredient. The next pair to speak was Paul and Hannah. It turned out that I wasn't the only one who had designs on one of Martin's proposals.

Paul spoke on their behalf.

"Hannah and I also have more than one project. Unfortunately one of them is the same as one of the three Martin just outlined. First and foremost we are focused on funding for startups from groups like ours, those of us who are on either fringe of the labour market, trying to get in or trying to stay in. We did meet with the two bankers with limited interest. Neither of them was encouraging, but because I'm a seasoned accountant with a business background both agreed to at least look at some of the ventures with which we develop relationships. The venture capitalist was even less interested. He didn't mince words: there is no way we can meet his lending criteria. We just can't offer the return he needs. However, he did make a good suggestion, actually one that Hannah already made but I dismissed out of ignorance. He felt that we should take a serious look at building a crowdfunding platform for senior and youth startups. That's where we're headed and we will be submitting a more detailed outline tomorrow. We strongly support the idea of establishing an incubator for non-tech ventures as a launch pad for companies trying to make it in the traditional economy. What we want from that initiative is the opportunity to become the funding specialist to assist in that project.

"As for our second concept we feel that we are the right ones to pursue the business brokerage idea focused on solving business succession issues for retiring owners who need to get their equity out of viable businesses rather than dumping them on a cold market. I appreciate Martin's interest in this area, but we feel that he and Dominic should pick one of his other two projects or both. Business brokerage is really a financial issue with a host of tax implications. As an accountant with good relationships in the profession this is a natural for me. Since Hannah is immersed in an MBA program she has great contacts for capable aspiring business owners who can bring synergy to the table as well. Don't you agree, Sam?"

Sam was delighted with the prospect of competition in one of his pet areas of underdeveloped opportunity, but he had no intention of making a choice between competing groups.

"Well, Paul, I see merit in both proposals. Either you work together or you both make your best case tomorrow. Ultimately I can't keep either of you from going ahead, so if you can't agree the market will decide who's best equipped."

Paul was a little dismayed at the answer. He'd been sure his professional designation would win the day. Sam didn't commiserate and moved on to see what Jake and Andrea had planned. Their revised group had no senior or at least we thought it didn't but they had recruited one who was about to speak on their behalf. Margaret stood up to take the floor.

"Jake and Andrea came to me for help last night. After listening to their plan I'm throwing in with them. Our plan is different than the first two. We are counting on an incubator coming out of one of our groups. We want to be the first venture that joins that incubator. Our project is to open an adult daycare service. It was Andrea's idea. It seems their grandmother lives with Andrea, Dominic, and the rest of the family. She's become a serious couch potato. Andrea's parents both work, and since Andrea's been waitressing at night the responsibility of watching her grandmother during the day has fallen to her. It's a big job that is not understood, not appreciated, and not valued. What it is, however, is a critical need for the elderly. They need activities and stimulation. Their adult children need reliable options to care for them during the work day. That's the service we will provide. We're operating on the same premise as any daycare for children; we will provide a reliable program designed to fill a growing need.

"Andrea has already started feeling out recruits by word of mouth, especially among recent graduates that she knows who have been frustrated getting their careers off the ground. So far we have interest from a male nurse, a physiotherapist, and some amateur entertainers who want to work with aging seniors. All of them are desperate to get some work experience that's relevant to their education. We also have a retired librarian interested on a volunteer basis. I'd like to stress this is not a health care project — at least not physical health. It may well be a terrific program to promote extended mental health. This is a social program that I feel I can get behind. I have already started working with municipal staff to make sure we clear all the necessary hurdles quickly.

"Jake took a phone survey this morning of about twenty homeowners that have an older relative living with them. We got most of the names here last night just by asking around in the Legion. Fifteen of them want to meet with us to discuss the service. We are following the mandate of a lean startup by getting feedback from our market upfront as we design the service and well before we start it.

"I am very impressed by the initiative shown by Jake and Andrea. It's rejuvenating to work with them; so much energy and determination. One thing we will need is space, and we plan to meet with Nick and Doris to discuss possibilities after the happy hour."

Just about everyone outside their group was taken completely off guard. First by Margaret's shift into the group — we had seen them talking but thought she was just offering advice — and secondly by the amount of progress this group had made in such a short time. Sam made no attempt to hide his surprise as he asked the obvious question:

"Does this mean that your interest in social entrepreneurship in general and education in particular is off the table?"

"Actually," said Margaret, "I have a short presentation on that as well."

Margaret was turning into a rock star. Maybe I'd underestimated her as a politician.

"Revitalizing the Home and School program is ambitious, but it still needs to be done. I'm meeting with a few teachers next week to get input. Once I have that I'll do some testing on parents. It's a serious challenge. Parents have so little free time, but the system is vulnerable and private school is not the only solution for parents who care. If things go well when I announce in September that I'm not running for re-election, I can use that platform to get publicity for the Home and School initiative and for the elder day care centre.

"I do have one other idea on education though. Sam, you've pointed out often enough that entrepreneurial thinking is becoming far more critical, especially for young people. If the incubator goes forward I want whoever orchestrates it to allow for co-op students from both the community college and secondary school to get involved. They offer voluntary labour for experience and I'm sure that would be a win-win situation. That's all I have to report."

Sam was generous in his praise.

"Margaret, you have really astounded me as has your whole team. I'm used to action-oriented entrepreneurs who get results. The last type of person I would have expected to make a lightning-speed adjustment in that direction is a retiring politician. Congratulations to you and your team members. Well done! I guess that means we move on to Nick, which I believe is where this whole thing started."

Margaret was quite an act to follow but the juices were flowing so I was anxious to start.

"Well, it looks like Andrea made a good decision when she moved off my team yesterday. But it seems Doris has made a good one for her and for me. We have space to rent, use, donate, all depending on the structure of what ventures are created. One thing for sure is we want to take the lead on the incubator project. Space to work, brainstorm, receive mentoring, and so on is the foundation of any incubator. Accelerators are different, but what we're trying to build here requires nurturing and stability, not just speed. I respect Martin's interest, and perhaps we can involve him in some way, but we want that critical development under our umbrella. We also want you involved, Sam, as our definitive advisor. Doris and I are going to acquire more space dedicated to developing successful ventures. We will act as the property managers of all of them, allowing Doris to use her considerable skills in that area. I want to be active in the mentoring and advisory board activities, which I suspect is where Martin has interest. We need you to be *our* mentor, Sam, and to help build up the network of advisors that we'll need to make this work. No government money is a commitment we need to follow, just as Brent has done with Tech Engagement.

"So, Sam, everyone else has spoken. I know you. I know that you have been developing a vision for this enterprise. Don't you think you should share your foresight with us?"

Sam had that same innocent look on his face that he had years ago when he threw that football as far down the hill as he could and made me chase it.

"Well, I've made you wait all week so I guess I can share a few suggestions if you like. Remember, this is a work in progress. It has been since Nick first suggested a series focused on seniors. For me this whole exercise is about integration, about bringing complementary strengths together to deal with some glaring weaknesses. It's the ultimate test of team building because it involves bringing people together who on the surface are not likeminded at all and who are competing in the same labour market. On top of that, the labour market is broken right now and nobody wants to talk about the reasons. I'm not prepared to go too far with my thoughts today. Really you are doing just great in doing what I've asked. But it's time that you became the architects of your collective futures. I'll give you a general overview of what I feel can be accomplished here; the rest is up to you.

Regardless, don't walk out of here after tomorrow with any delusions that your problems are solved. If you take this project on it's going to be difficult. Like any venture into entrepreneurship you will never work harder for less in the first year. The good news is that all of your ideas can be incorporated into this project and more. I have no doubt of that. The immediate challenge starting right now is to wrestle responsibilities and entitlements to the ground and focus on building the best possible structure, one that rewards people properly and allows each of you the opportunity that you're looking for. That's all possible and I'll do my best to shepherd you through that process.

"We started with a problem. There was no effective support system in place for you. It's beyond ambition to think that you can create one. Anyway, I've given a name to this budding enterprise, one that I think encapsulates everything I believe you can accomplish here. If you're onboard, welcome to *The Age Alliance*! It's yours to define or reject. You have twenty-four hours to negotiate and consolidate who does what and decide if this is worth pursuing. Tomorrow afternoon we'll all know if we're daydreaming or not. Congratulations on your progress so far, but the work is just starting.

"I don't know about you, but I can use a drink. Happy hour starts in ten minutes."

CHAPTER TWENTY

The Mentoring Mind

There was no time to bask in the glow of Sam's praise. We had a lot to consider and our last speaker of the series was ready and waiting; the most prominent one yet. Sam had brought in Badri Gupta, an experienced mentor and venture capitalist from one of the foremost accelerator programs in Silicon Valley. Mr. Gupta was in Toronto for a conference that started on Monday. Somehow Sam had persuaded him to come out and share his experiences with a rag-tag bunch of aspiring entrepreneurs who were far removed from the tech genius types that competed so vigorously just to get his attention. All of us had heard of him so he really needed no introduction. Sam kept it short, referring to him as the *guru of mentoring*. Fortunately for us Mr. Gupta had an affinity for underdogs.

"Sam tells me that you're trying something new and different here. That's exciting, but it's also going to be hard work. If you're going to succeed you have a lot to learn and even more to teach. Business coaching has become a growth industry, but I believe that Sam has more in mind for you than that. Coaches generally focus on getting short-term results. More often than not they work with established businesses that have specific problems. Mentoring is very different, usually beginning in the startup stage and taking a long-term approach, nurturing the protégée through periods of growth. What Sam is proposing here by combining seniors loaded with experience but new to entrepreneurship with young, raw talent is fairly unique and a serious business experiment. Incubators and accelerators are springing up almost daily, but this does seem different. Those of you who are seniors will have a natural tendency to teach, combined with a compelling need to learn. Getting the juniors to listen will not be difficult. Feeding of their energy will sustain the drive you need to succeed. There is no better classroom than the business world and no more willing student than an aspiring entrepreneur coming off a series of barriers to getting started, regardless of age. So here are some key elements for you to consider.

"Business coaching is not regulated, nor is mentoring. Anyone can set up shop as a business coach. One of the redeeming qualities of incubators is shared experience. What you learn this week can be shared next. With that in mind, the juniors here will soon be mentoring along with their older, more experienced, associates putting the rigours of a startup into perspective for your new ventures as they come onside. If you want to be taken seriously as an organization that mentors effectively, you'll also need to bring in a strong cast of outsiders who are leaders, like Sam, to supplement your own strengths — business people with extensive experience. You must have strong additional outside mentors for you and for your ventures. The whole world is trying to teach entrepreneurship, but there is no proven system or method to do it. Experience is critical. Sharing experiences with an effective mentor can save time, prevent mistakes, and help ensure success. That's what you hope to offer. Never underestimate the value of a critical eye from a seasoned veteran.

"Coaches hold hands and ask a lot of questions. The answer to the questions and the solutions for many problems lie with the business owner. Coaches help find a solution within your own knowledge and skill set. They will never know as much as you do about your business but they know how to lead you to a solution.

Mentors build knowledge. They prepare you for the path ahead by adding to what you know based on what they've experienced. Looking to the past helps anticipate the future. Mentoring involves fostering development while coaching means drawing from within one's internal data bank. It's a subtle difference but important. A mentor is an advisor and teacher. Someone who inspires, motivates, educates, and encourages. A coach fills a different need, offering a pep talk for you to do what you already know but have been ignoring. By all means some coaches engage in mentoring but overall the approach is different, focused more on short-term results, immediate solutions, and less on long-range potential and personal development. If you build this 'Age Alliance' that Sam has suggested, you'll engage in both, at least I hope that you will.

"Mentoring is best served by remaining outside the business, divorced from day-to-day pressures but made available on a regular basis such as monthly meetings. Setting benchmarks is a very effective way to achieve results through mentoring. A period of separation allows the person being mentored to achieve some targeted result and measure progress. A break allows those being mentored to evolve and mature. Because of this element of detachment information has to flow both ways. The mentor is also a sounding board. Every entrepreneur needs one. Mentors have to be excellent listeners, obviously for advice, but even more to let others rant and vent frustrations. You have to be an active listener. Are you? Take notes. Ask questions. Mirror back to make sure you've understood correctly. Mentoring is an interactive process based on common bonds and mutual commitment. Mentors are dedicated to the success of their pupil. If not they won't be effective. Coaches get results. Mentors build character in those who will continue to get results long after the mentoring ends.

"Mentoring itself is an entrepreneurial activity grounded in problem solving, absolved of prison thinking, dependent on an open mind, committed to results, observant of opportunity, embracing a willingness to step outside the box and be diligent to a fault. Mentors act responsibly, are respectful of those that they mentor, and are always ready to offer advice. Being a mentor will improve your understanding of your skills as you reflect on your experience, seeking improvement to gain a different perspective on your achievements, recognizing different reasons for your success. It is critical that you understand the landscape and the organization you are guiding, not just the principal with whom you deal. Effective mentoring is a very satisfying role dependent on building a special trust relationship.

It also depends on your ability to forewarn about a whole range of outside developments that may influence the business. You must never forget that as a mentor you are leading a leader who is immersed in his or her venture and is vulnerable to being blindsided by external factors. The relationship has to be a two-way street. The person who you mentor must be receptive to change, willing to take action, and be open to ideas. If you can build this type of relationship you will be effective and the reward will come from recognizing that you've had a profound effect on others, which multiplies out as your principal grows — teaches and builds a team that produces a strong organization that will continue to grow and mature in your absence. These ideas are all generalities, but they establish the framework you will need. Once you get more involved with specifics the excitement and satisfaction will multiply provided you stay within the guidelines we've just discussed. I wish you nothing but success and I look forward to coming back in a few years to see how the Age Alliance has matured. Thanks for inviting me here to see what you're doing."

Things were moving quickly. We had leapfrogged from mentee to mentor in what seemed like a millisecond. We had moved from listening to an eighteen-year-old describe his startup experience as a fifteen-year-old to having one of the best-known venture capitalists in the tech world mentor us on mentoring. The experience was absolutely surreal. Is it possible that all of this happened in just five days?

Well, the sixth day was looming and there were many things to be decided, at least in principle. All of us were evaluating options. I felt like a dearth of opportunity had evolved into a wealth of potential. At least we had the possibility of becoming a real team, a diverse group that I now saw collectively featured considerable strength.

Follow-up activities would go on that night and in the morning but the hard core negotiations would have to involve Sam. Just the name "The Age Alliance" was uplifting and it was on everyone's tongue as we headed home to share progress stories with our families. Sam went with me but still kept silent. I really wanted him to step up and mentor me right then and there but he made me wait. I should never have chased down that football so long ago. The pattern had been set and was now established. He knew what was going on. I was doing what I was told, at least for a little longer.

CHAPTER TWENTY-ONE

Defining the Alliance

Sam had chosen his name carefully. When I looked up the word "alliance" in my thesaurus alternative words included association, coalition, union, co-operation, agreement, bond, and pact. All of them implied a separate but equal status of sorts, at least to me. That was certainly what I wanted. In reality, I didn't know any of the others well enough, with the possible exception of Doris, which was working to my benefit and hers. Making any financial commitment in the form of a legal partnership was not going to happen. I doubted any of the seniors in the group would feel differently. Sam had defined entrepreneurship as self-determination, taking control of your business and your life. I was ready to do that which did not imply being in the minority within a larger group. An association or coalition was more acceptable. We should have the basis for that. There was a community of interest; that was undeniable. The sessions this week were a baptism under fire of sorts and were built on a common bond forged out of necessity. There seemed to be enough diversity in the venture ideas presented so far to suggest that we could all control our own operations under the umbrella of this alliance. Having separate interests made sense. Defining what each of those individual interests should be under the umbrella of an alliance was more demanding.

My biggest concern was disputes over leading specific areas. I wanted the incubator as part of my mandate. Martin was the main challenge, but I was determined to ward him off.

Doris and I met in the morning. We agreed that the incubator should be under our control. Since we had space available, that seemed to give us the upper hand in our upcoming negotiation. Providing space was a prime function of any incubator. Martin didn't have any comparable advantage to offer. Both of us felt he wanted to invest in startups more than advise them. To make sure that we could box him out we defined a progressive program that would enhance the incubator *and* help us secure tenants. Somehow I had to make sure that I spoke before Martin so we could deflect his momentum by presenting our complete plan.

I was anxious to get started but we were all waiting for Sam. Doris had picked me up in the morning so Sam had my car. The mood in the room was one of cautious optimism. Collectively it appeared that we'd created opportunity in a meaningful way. The pie was large enough for all of us. Would greed get in the way? I'd considered that. Were Doris and I acting in self-interest or were we really offering the best alternative for the program and the group? It was hard to be objective, but I felt that we had merit on our side. Where was Sam? Finally he arrived with just two minutes to spare. My theory was that he didn't want any discussion in advance. He didn't allow any and started right into the topic at hand.

"So we've reached the last day, one that's pivotal. There are a number of proposals on the table, most of which seem sound, or at least worth pursuing. There is some overlap, the pros and cons of which need to be debated today. We've introduced a framework and an umbrella concept that is unique. I hope you've come prepared to compromise for the greater good of the project. Right now I want to discuss the concept briefly before we start.

"You know when I wrote my book on entrepreneurship it was targeted to the average Joe. That's who I'm concerned about; people like you with ability that don't or won't believe entrepreneurship possible. Ironically the book was embraced by the academic community and through them found its way into tech circles. These are the people who have the opportunities and all the tools they need. Despite their advantages they need exposure and mentoring on the fundamentals, so the book was well received. Still, my main goal has been to better prepare and encourage development and diversity in the traditional economy. Even the recent MBA grad can't write his or her ticket anymore. Initial salaries are declining. In contrast, a little short-term pain as part of a startup team can make for much larger longer-term gain made feasible through entrepreneurship. Multinational companies will continue to grow through acquisition. Build and sell is a viable success strategy. You've heard me say this many times this week. The tech community has developed infrastructure and systems to sustain their own. Call it an ecosystem or just the venture capital mindset, whatever you wish, but there's no comparable framework for those in the traditional economy. There are incubators of some kind in many communities, but usually there's some tech connection. There's both a need and an opportunity for something more ambitious. For sure some of the tech approach does spill over into applications for mainstream businesses, but by and large the everyday entrepreneur who wants to start a service business is on their own with no investors lined up to consider them or offer them startup capital, and no incubator to nurse them over the gestation period required to launch. Much of the current tech dialogue revolves around scalability — building massive companies reflecting the build and sell mentality or in the case of extreme success a build and acquire strategy. Sorry, but those options are unlikely for most of us.

"As a result, even in this new era where the prevailing factors in the labour market push every one of us toward entrepreneurship, the concept is only flying high in the tech sector. Outside the tech sphere we're starting fewer businesses. In that sense entrepreneurship is in decline, when for individuals the need to embrace it has risen significantly. This is not the age of capitalism that many think. We are in an age of corporatism where large companies dominate and individual rewards and opportunities are in decline unless you reach the top of the pyramid and join the ranks of the super-rich. Capitalism rewards results at all levels, letting the free market decide who, how, and why. Corporatism interferes with market forces and market choices. In this environment we need to build support systems for the average guy who's under duress, facing declining opportunity, job instability, and limitations on upward mobility. That's what I hope will come out of the Age Alliance: a local support system for the shoulder groups, old and young alike. Maybe it will even become a model for others to follow.

"So I have my naive and idealistic goals and expectations about what we can resolve today. Ambitious to be sure, but I know what can be accomplished if you're determined to do it. My opinion only matters if you buy into the process. Nothing will come of this if you can't structure a concept that will work for all of you. Finding your future has been our goal this week and any greater meaning that comes out of this process only happens as a result of achieving that. There are only a few people who get to do something unique that has impact on a huge number of people. Right now as far as entrepreneurship is concerned the tech community has staked out that ground in the global economy. What I would love to see come out of this experience is taking the tech model and doing it differently for a broader audience. Whatever we decide today won't make you billionaires, but it could set an example that can be replicated in many other areas, provided we do it right. So who wants to go first?"

I was on my feet before anyone else, determined to outline what Doris and I had discussed. I wanted to manage that incubator with all its challenges and needed to show it before Martin.

"Sam, our group fully supports the principles of the Age Alliance and we hope it will be exactly that — an alliance of distinct age groups consolidating a complete range of services operated independently under the guidance of a founding council made up of all of us, including you if you'll do it. Doris and I want to focus on the space requirements and we want to manage the incubator. Providing mentoring is a separate question and we hope the council will take the lead on that aspect. Our commitment is to provide five thousand square feet of open office area at no charge where startups can begin the ventures. That will include a meeting room that the ventures can book and a common lunch room. Last night I spoke to my previous employer, which is in the process of moving the business back to the States. They've donated all their office equipment for our project, which includes a ton of desks, filing cabinets, and so on. Each venture will be given a year in the space to get started. Beyond that we hope to fill my building and maybe acquire other buildings to provide space for the next stage of their evolution at 20 percent below market value for a five-year period, provided they sign a ten-year lease and the last five years will be at market value. In return for these concessions we will receive a 3 percent equity position in the company, protected against dilution. Unlike the tech model we want the Age Alliance to develop a mentorship program that encourages these companies to focus on generating revenue as early as possible, becoming self-sufficient in the process. By subsidizing their space requirements we hope to bring them to viability early on.

"We met with Margaret, Jake, and Andrea last night and subject to what transpires here today we've agreed on the terms for a ten-year lease on five thousand square feet. That gives their venture into elder care six months free rent plus the 20 percent reduction for five years. They also have the first right of refusal on an adjoining five thousand feet.

"I know there is disagreement about roles within this alliance. Martin feels our incubator should be his to run, but I think his talents and needs are best met elsewhere, hopefully within the umbrella you've laid out. Doris and I are anxious to see how others see themselves fitting into this structure, but space is an important ingredient and we wanted to make our position clear by establishing a foundation for further discussion."

As I looked around the room I sensed a general mood of agreement. That was a relief. People were engaged. Negotiations like this are tough. Unilateral concessions made that result in an upside for those that make them are always viewed with suspicion. I was counting on Sam to follow through on his assertion that this project had to give us what each of us needed as well as working on merit as a benefit for the others. I didn't look at Martin but I thought I could feel his eyes glaring at me. Naturally he was the next to speak. His first words caught me off guard.

"I agree with Nick, he and Doris should manage the incubator. Dominic and I discussed this at length last night. Mr. Gupta clarified a few issues for us. Our principal goal is not to become mentors on the outside looking in. We want to participate in some of the ventures actively in a management role. Not every one of them, we will be selective. We want to be the catalyst that promotes and invests in startups right here, practicing the lean startup mindset. Our efforts will be to recruit ventures for the incubator. At the same time both of us need to build revenue, so we're going to start our service brokerage immediately. I guess that makes us the second startup for the Alliance, offering everything from cleaning to accounting to personal shopping. If the same offer that you gave the elder care centre is open Nick, we'll take three thousand square feet and maybe a couple of those old desks. I also want to sit on the council that Nick suggested. As I see it. We're all cofounders of the Age Alliance. Beyond that Dominic and I are withdrawing our idea on the business brokerage idea to deal with business succession in favour of Paul and Hannah taking on that role. What we will be doing is trying to recruit young people for that program as well and possibly getting involved with some of those ventures if investors are required. There's plenty of meat for us to go after in this alliance. Now, Dominic wants to make his own announcement."

Despite being a generation apart, the two of them were very much alike; neither one shied away from an opinion while both seemed to see opportunity better than most. The idea that they wanted to be on the inside of some of the ventures in an active way seemed to be a good fit and it didn't surprise any of us. In fact, having willing investors brought an essential venture capital element to the alliance. We needed people who were willing to invest even limited amounts of money along with considerable sweat equity to take an active role.

Dominic was all smiles as he stood to speak with a surprising degree of confidence.

"Martin and I talked well into the night. We agreed that my role is to recruit youth entrepreneurs with a venture plan to join the incubator while he'll focus on the service brokerage. I will work full time in the brokerage in the summer and on weekends, recruiting other students as well. Beyond that he's convinced me to follow through on my acceptance at the Rotman School of Management at the University of Toronto and enroll in the commerce program. When I graduate I'll join him full time."

Andrea let out an audible gasp at Dominic's announcement, apparently unaware of what her brother was going to say. Martin was beaming. Maybe there was a little more of the mentor in him than he was prepared to admit. The day was full of surprises, which were far from over.

Next Hanna took the floor on behalf of herself and Paul. She had started the week as a reluctant participant, coming out just to please her grandmother. Now she was far removed from Margaret's plans and deeply immersed in her own.

"Paul and I have been studying the options available to fund the kind of ventures likely to find a home in the Age Alliance. We want to become the principal financing arm and we like crowdfunding. We know that we can work with the banks on a limited basis, but that's unlikely in the early stages of these startups. Venture capital is out of the question because we can't offer the returns that can come from a successful tech startup. We want to extend the idea of the Age Alliance to the funding market. We want to focus on raising smaller amounts from people like us who need a return but can only risk smaller amounts of their assets. That means retirees and young people. Crowdfunding works best when consumers who use the products invest in expanding the future of that business. We feel this logic will work very well for Age Alliance ventures, attracting investments from young and old alike. That's where we intend to focus our efforts. Plus we're going ahead full speed with the matching process involved in placing young people in established business to build a succession plan and negotiate achievable buyouts. Martin and Dominic gave us a heads up that they were withdrawing from that area. Thanks for that. Paul's already started researching businesses in the area that seem to be facing succession issues. We feel that will be an important source of revenue for us. Both Paul and I are in a good position to bootstrap and take very little out of our new company for a year or more. It's our intention to reach an agreement with Nick and Doris as well so that the entire alliance can be housed in the same location."

It seemed that everyone had done their homework and some serious soul searching. There had been more dialogue than I realized. My position as landlord had pretty much been assumed by all. That left one group to speak. It was Jake who rose to represent them. Jake hadn't said much of anything on the first day, but he was a changed man now.

"Margaret insisted that I do the talking since elder care was my suggestion. Andrea deserves most of the credit for our progress because she had the responsibility of looking after her grandmother all day. Sam told us that most opportunities start with a problem. That's what got us thinking. Andrea had the problem and many others have the same one. Elder daycare will solve a problem for a lot of people. Last night Margaret recruited some retired teachers to work with us, including a music teacher, so Nick's building will be rocking before you know it. Andrea and

I have applied for the summer program that David Saxon used so we hope to have some seed capital to help us. Beyond that we intend to work with Paul and Hannah to raise funds. We will be operational this fall and we're planning to start taking reservations and deposits by the end of the month. We have to get our pricing right, but we already have customers asking to be put on a wait list. I guess that's about it for us. Quite a change in a week, but then Sam has a record for making things happen in a short time. I'd just like to thank you Sam. This week's been an eye opener."

There was no disagreement. Heads were still spinning, mine among them. Margaret was the only one left to speak, but she declined to add anything about her education initiatives. That would come later. At the moment she was engrossed in the elder care venture. Things had gone full circle and we were back to Sam.

"Jake said it quite well; this week has been a revelation, even for me. When Nick approached me less than two weeks ago we didn't contemplate anything like this. Once he started to recruit I started thinking about what might be possible through co-operation. The techies do it. They re-energize each other. If you've ever spent any time in a tech incubator environment there's plenty of evidence of friendly competition and mutual support. That's why I decided to bring in some young blood to complement our seniors. So the real question is can you nurture that kind of support right here, for anyone in any form of entrepreneurial endeavour, young or old or somewhere in between?

"Most people would not have thought this kind of intergenerational collaboration possible. Most would say 'why try this,' to which my response is 'why not try it?' I will sit on your council, but I will be Mr. Gupta's classic type of mentor, on the outside looking in. As a group you must sustain the drive to make this work. It will not be easy. You will work the long hours. You will build the support teams. There are a ton of potential mentors in your local retirement community. All of them are eminently qualified, and believe me, they want to be recruited. There is no better way to feel useful while validating your career in the process. We have only scratched the surface of what is possible. As you build graduates of the program the possibilities will multiply. Some of them will become your most effective mentors. I congratulate all of you on a truly successful week. But it's almost time for our last happy hour and a well-deserved celebratory drink together.

"Just before we do let's step back and debrief for a moment. What has surprised you the most this week, good or bad?"

Dominic led off, still flushed with enthusiasm.

"I can't believe the confidence that I've gained in such a short time. My decision to go to Rotman seems like a no-brainer now. I would never have believed that I could have such fun, productive discussions with Martin or any of the older people here."

Andrea, who began the week as a committed cynic, reinforced her brother's comment.

"I can't believe the opportunities that we've flushed out. My life just seemed so bleak last week. I almost didn't come for this."

Martin injected with a thought that I certainly shared.

"I needed some excitement and enthusiasm. Once I got Dominic started I couldn't slow him down. What if … what if … what if … I needed that injection of energy."

Paul agreed.

"That's what I enjoyed the most. Hannah and I called it idea ping pong because we had such different perspectives, but once we married up our ideas things began to look possible."

Even Jake wanted to add his two cents.

"When we started I felt that you guys wouldn't take me seriously. What surprised me the most was the acceptance and the open dialogue that we've had. You made that happen, Sam, but I didn't see it coming at all."

Doris was next.

"The young people gave me a sense of purpose. I came just trying to find a way to survive and play out the string until I could retire. I have a very different outlook now. Margaret and I discussed it this morning. We were both surprised by the respect and responsiveness to our ideas. Margaret loved working with Jake and Andrea."

"Indeed I did," said Margaret. "It's just been great to get past the infighting of council and deal with young people who want to accomplish something meaningful. I've learned that most of us are far too cynical about millennials and their abilities."

The last comment was left for me.

"I'm not sure surprise is the right word. Disbelief might be more appropriate. All of us came here looking for a lifeline. Now we're launching a support system based on location and age, determined to create opportunity right here in our local community, a program focused on solving our problems and offering solutions to others just like us. Unbelievable! The combined talent in this room and in this community is a powerhouse that we simply didn't recognize. I suppose that's true of most communities. There's a ton of work to do but I can hardly wait to get started. All I can add is thanks Sam. Now can I buy you a drink?"

And so with a round of enthusiastic applause, the last session ended and a whole series of new careers began.

CHAPTER TWENTY-TWO

The End of the Beginning

As we broke up and went for that drink, I had the sharp twinge of a reality check. Now what? What the hell were we thinking? A week ago we were tripping over our shoelaces, stumbling around looking for any opportunity, but now, just seven days later, we were planning to mentor others and foster the growth of entrepreneurship in our community. Were we delusional? Sam called us ambitious, now that was an understatement. It was double rum and Coke for me but everyone else seemed oblivious to the gravity of our new collective commitment. I started into these sessions plagued by doubt and struggling to find ideas to fill up one building. Now I was giving away free space and contemplating buying more buildings. Plus I had a new partner who needed an immediate income of some type. The weight of responsibility was a burden. Yet when I considered the specifics I was confident that I could pull it off and that felt good. I just knew we would find a way to make this happen. Still, right at that moment my mind was an enigma, a paradox, plagued by inconsistency.

Everyone else seemed oblivious to any sense of foreboding. Drinks were flowing. Conversations were animated. Passion was the dominant emotion. Laughter was the pervading sound in the room. It seemed like utter chaos to me. As I started to order another double, Sam sat down beside me.

"Not too deep in thought, are you Nicky? Forget it for tonight. I know what you're feeling. It's the responsibility. I feel it every time I complete one of these programs. My protégés always end on a positive note. That's one of my principal goals. For most of them anything and everything seems possible. That's what it means to be a leader of a team that believes in you, a team that is motivated because you took a chance. A few of us look past the thoughts of success and focus on the fear of failure. I can read it in your eyes. Right now you feel sick to your stomach. It will get worse over the next twenty-four hours. Then your mind will engage. Determination will kick in and you'll start adding ideas to the long list of things that must be done to succeed. Next the thoughts of failure will recede as you immerse yourself in the process of entrepreneurship. Your office will have a revolving door as your associates bring you a constant stream of problems. You will sink or swim, either thriving on the constant flow of challenges or drowning in your inability to deal with them. I'll put my money on thriving. Anyway, let's talk about something more important — you owe me a couple of hot dogs at Gino's. I'm starving!"

Sam paid the bar bill and we moved to say our goodbyes to the group. All of them were effusive with praise for Sam and thanks to me for pulling the seminar series together. Sam received an enthusiastic hug from each and every one of them. I suggested that we should meet at my building on Monday morning to get things moving. Everyone but Sam agreed to be there.

"Don't worry, I'm only a phone call or a train ride away. You don't need handholding. You've shown that by your responses all week. It's time to get your feet wet. As your principal mentor I'm advising you to appoint Nick chairman of your council. You need a spokesman and someone to set the agenda."

Surprisingly, everyone accepted the idea with enthusiasm, something else for me to worry about on Sunday.

Then the two of us were on our own, headed for our comfort zone at Gino's. The trip itself went by in silence. Both of us had a lot on our minds. As we sat in the car gobbling down two twelve-inch hot dogs each, our own extra-thick milkshakes, plus sharing a large order of onion rings, I relaxed. My mind wandered back to the conversation we'd had right there two weeks before. Sam had been right about Gino. He probably was the first entrepreneur that we'd known when we were growing up. Like Sam I remembered Gino encouraging us to stay in school and not to be like him. Gino always made time to talk. Whenever I went back as an adult he always asked me how business was going, often making comparisons to his own little hot dog stand. Without a doubt he was guiding me without my realizing it. He always had a story about his business that related to any problem I mentioned. The stories always helped. I thought of them as a diversion, but often the message kick-started a solution for me. All the time I thought it was me working my way through the problems on my own; Gino's was just the place I went for lunch when I needed to think. So that was mentoring, or was it coaching? At that point I didn't care. Life was good. My friendship with Sam was back on track. My opportunities were many. I now perceived the world as limitless. I had just gained a strong team of associates.

But most of all, the hot dogs were damn good!

EPILOGUE

May 11, 2015

It's appropriate that I should be back at the train station waiting for Sam to arrive. The monthly meeting of the Age Alliance council is on for this afternoon. Sam is bringing out two new observers who are interested in running satellite programs that parallel ours.

We have survived. Along the way we've flirted with becoming a creative success and financial failure, but we keep dodging the bullet. After periods of uplifting support resulting from great local and social media coverage, tons of encouragement, and an overwhelming number of applicants, none of which made us viable, we are gaining traction on every front. Although praise is a heady stimulant you can't run a car on fumes or a business or vanity.

We have all learned more than expected and as a result our lives have changed dramatically. Margaret did step down as mayor and now alternates between spending time advocating for students and seniors. She has become the Don Quixote of the local education system, taking a run at a whole range of issues, and she is the public face and vocal champion of the successful elder daycare program, our first startup. The rest of us rise and fall with the Age Alliance.

In the past two months Doris and I have signed up two established businesses as tenants, both for warehousing. We now have an adequate rent roll to pay Doris a salary and meet all other expenses. As for me, I can wait for things to happen, and they are starting to happen. Our incubator is thriving in terms of interest, but more importantly we have at least three new businesses beginning to generate revenue. That's become the stated number one goal for the Age Alliance to sustain itself: our ventures have to achieve short-term sustainability through revenue generation. Profitability may take longer, but sales are the life's blood of viability. If we don't see the possibility of early sales, we don't accept them. Our ventures cannot survive on the speculative bubble that feeds tech startups. We've raised our standards after learning the hard way that need is not enough. The founders have to be committed and the ventures have to pass a rigid viability analysis. If we reject them they get one more chance to modify their concept to make it more viable and resubmit. There is no sure thing, but speculation is not an illusion we can afford. Initially we took anyone that applied. With limited space and a pressing need to push these startups to generate revenue we had to toughen up. We almost lost Martin from the program because of his overzealous commitment to invest. He made two misguided investments in initial applicants, and both floundered. Now he's raised his standards. Believe it or not, none of our founding group has dropped out, although Doris also came close for financial reasons when she had to dip into her savings.

Jake and Andrea have had the most success with the elder daycare, one of those basic ideas that no one else recognized. Of course, if you ask anyone now, it should have been obvious that the program would work. Jake and Andrea are thriving and they're looking seriously at taking over additional space for the fall.

Martin and Dominic's service brokerage struggled over the winter, but Dominic has recruited some talented students who have helped with door-to-door promotion so the summer looks promising.

After the two misfires, Martin has invested in one of our three promising startups who are starting to produce revenue. Martin provided critical introductions to some of their key potential customers which accelerated progress. He did the same for one of the other ventures even though he didn't invest because of limited funds. All of this has helped our reputation.

I forgot to mention that Dominic has been acing his courses at Rotman and he frequently mentions continuing to the MBA program as a possibility. His involvement in the Age Alliance gives him a unique perspective.

Paul and Hannah were prepared to go lean and mean, which is a good thing because they have needed to bootstrap. So far they have placed aspiring young owners in two local firms for which the owner-operator is approaching retirement. The problem is that their fee will come far down the road, if and when the deal is done and when the earn-out purchase price is paid. They're currently working to establish a more practical fee schedule starting with an advance payable at the initial placement.

They have also been nursing along their crowdfunding network, waiting for our ventures to mature. A surprising number of seniors are looking for opportunity to get a higher return. Interest rates are low, and many of them don't trust the stock market. All of this puts more emphasis on us to focus on viability and early revenue generation. Our ventures need to succeed. One in ten, the reality for venture capitalists, just won't fly for our community. We are almost there. When we go to our crowd, we will be offering a sound option catered to seniors who need limited diversification and young people who are willing to take a managed risk. The idea of an age alliance extends to our investors. The timing is good. Hannah has just graduated from her MBA program and is ready to plunge into our funding program full time. Paul is hoping for some cash flow this year. Aren't we all?

As for Sam, well Sam is Sam. He has written two more books and he's still doing regular webinars. I see him monthly for our council meetings and when we can we end up at Gino's.

And then there's me. My grandson arranged for me to talk to his high school entrepreneurship class once a month. I've also arranged a co-op program with the local community college. Life is good. One year can be a short time. One year can be an eternity. This past year has been both. I have never enjoyed myself more.

APPENDIX I

One-Line Wisdom from the Seminars of Sam Macleod

Sam Says:

1. It's not about the money.
2. Entrepreneurs are born, but they can also be made, developed, and nurtured.
3. Underestimating the competition is a reckless and unnecessary risk.
4. Indecision almost always leads to bad decisions.
5. The question must never be if a thing *can* be done but rather how it *will* be done.
6. Face the things you like least and find a way to do them.
7. Look for the opportunity when it arises, *not* when you need it.
8. Opportunities are not the mirror image of ideas.
9. Ask questions! Ask questions! Ask questions!
10. Entrepreneurship is a philosophy based on action.
11. The stability of government and society is critical for upward mobility.
12. Economics is a behavioural science. Fear and greed are the dominant emotions.
13. Greed leads to boom then bubble. Fear leads to bust.

14. One of the biggest reasons for small business failure is daydreaming at the start.
15. Don't confuse the perceptive nature of true genius with unattainable dreams.
16. Opportunities must be worthwhile and viable — forget the whimsical.
17. Rigidity in the banking systems is severely limiting small business.
18. Ground your business plan in reality. Take the emotion out of your thought process.
19. Pay yourself! Pay yourself! Pay yourself!
20. Commitment is one of the foundations of success.
21. The most dangerous person who can fool you about your own business is you.
22. Strive for success, defend against failure.
23. Things can go wrong, so negotiate to cover the downside.
24. There are no guarantees. Do your homework first, then trust your instincts.
25. When things do go wrong, the ability to adjust is your lifeline.
26. Never make a decision on the premise "I can stand the loss."
27. There is no such thing as entrepreneurial infallibility.
28. When you incur a tax loss, remember the word "tax" is just an adjective.
29. Never be satisfied with failure as the end game.
30. Small business is part of the global economy not a junior subset.
31. There will always be voids in the marketplace.
32. The global economy embodies change, which mandates flexibility.
33. Structural unemployment is best solved by entrepreneurs with a local bias.
34. Cultivate relationships in India and with likeminded entrepreneurs elsewhere.
35. No entrepreneur worth his salt is immune to self-doubt.
36. Free enterprise needs government to ensure opportunity.
37. Government needs the drive and efficiency of free enterprise to stay viable.

38. Countries, like any other entity, cannot be sustained by debt indefinitely.
39. Entrepreneurship of necessity is very different from entrepreneurship of opportunity.
40. Entrepreneurs of any stripe make things happen!
41. Entrepreneurs are agents of change — the principal catalysts of economic progress.
42. Overall, your business has to be fun. You have to like what you do.
43. Things that you don't like still have to be done, and on time!
44. Everything cannot be simple. Sometimes you have to study to understand.
45. Every problem is an opportunity.
46. Decisions must be delivered with authority, not uncertainty.
47. Don't confuse inventors or investors with entrepreneurs.
48. Know and understand your numbers.
49. Cash flow never lies.
50. Where expenditures are concerned: Payback rules!
51. Don't let your enthusiasm lead to commitments that make you vulnerable
52. Assume makes an "ass" of "u" and "me."
53. One set of assumptions is reckless.
54. There is no such thing as planning with certainty.
55. Projects can take twice as long, cost twice as much, and make half the profits we plan.
56. Make realism temper your enthusiasm, but don't lose your drive as a result.
57. Negotiation is a process that has to evolve.
58. Never enter into negotiation without being prepared. Understand the other side.
59. You can learn as much from your failures than from your success.
60. Most partnerships don't end well.
61. Merging business with family can work, but it can also compromise both.

62. Partners seldom agree how a business evolved or who made what contribution.
63. Salesmen are like halfbacks, getting the glory, but going nowhere without the team.
64. Relationships take work.
65. Creativity is the cornerstone of shameless self-promotion.
66. Never forget to ask for the order.
67. One good supplier can help you succeed with hundreds of good customers.
68. Relationships, creativity, and innovation are integrated and interdependent.
69. The electronic revolution levels the playing field for independent entrepreneurs.
70. Don't lose balance! Don't lose balance! Don't lose balance!
71. You have to work to live. There is no meaningful future in living to work.
72. Beware hyper connectivity — 24/7 is a recipe for disaster.
73. Don't make your business too big. It benefits everyone but you.
74. Don't let your business outgrow you.
75. Remember the crocodile farm — beware commitments that eat up your profits.
76. Entrepreneurs are self-starters.
77. There are people who make things happen, others who watch things happen, and many who wonder what happened.
78. Remember the "nation of shopkeepers" that built an empire.
79. You are a generalist, wearing every hat possible.
80. What you do pay yourself must be fair to you and your company.
81. Fair pay includes at least 10 percent that must be saved.
82. Income splitting is a right. Don't abuse it, but make sure you use it.
83. Keep your personal investments separate from your business. Balance.
84. Your business is not you.
85. Invest in yourself — seminars, trade shows. Payback is in your hands and your ideas.

86. Take vacations! Take vacations! Take vacations!
87. Be decisive — leaders are.
88. Develop pride of performance, not of position.
89. Be determined — leaders are.
90. Don't underestimate the power of confidence. Don't undermine it with ego.
91. Motivation — the fear of failure or the drive for success?
92. Greed leads to bad decisions.
93. You only pay tax if you make the money.
94. Never forget the inverse relationship between risk and reward.
95. Remember "Freedom 95."
96. Do you understand the meaning of "unlimited liability?"
97. Most entrepreneurial skills and experiences are transferable to new opportunities.
98. Don't go cheap on legal and accounting advice.
99. Like it or not, you do need a banker.
100. We live in a false economy.
101. "Too big to fail" subsidizes failure and encourages reckless behaviour.
102. We are in uncharted political and economic waters, featuring a crisis of leadership.
103. China-proof your business.
104. Don't build your plan based on growth/economic recovery — that's the upside.
105. Control the things you can and allow for the things you can't.
106. Having ideas makes you a dreamer — making those ideas happen converts you to an entrepreneur.
107. A plan is one possible outcome — the planning process provides a framework to anticipate and adjust.
108. Entrepreneurship is a life philosophy grounded in opportunity, fuelled by determination, and focused on results.
109. Growth is the life's blood for most entrepreneurs, but it can act like a python, exhausting your strengths and crushing your ability to survive.

110. For every innovation there are thousands of entrepreneurs who will find applications.

111. We only fail when we give up. Setbacks are part of the learning curve on the road to success.

112. Entrepreneurs love the process more than the project.

113. A successful entrepreneur relies on managed risk and measured success while avoiding reckless risk and failure.

114. There can only be one business that does something first. Finding ways to do it better and different adds many more paths to success.

115. Worrying is counterproductive. If the thing you're worrying about happens you've endured it twice, if it doesn't you've wasted time and energy worrying for nothing.

116. Failure is overrated: learn from it if you must, avoid it if you can.

117. Entrepreneurship takes many forms: the common bonds are the personal issues faced and the fundamental business challenges mastered.

118. Attracting investment can postpone the pursuit of the essential — profitability.

119. Self-deception creates a path to failure: an open mind molds the key to success.

120. Anticipation paves the road to solutions while preoccupation creates a roadblock to success.

121. Doubt is the forerunner of indecision, but confidence is the breeding ground for achievement.

122. If a problem can be solved with money it's not a problem.

123. The learning curve of an entrepreneur is forged from mistakes and setbacks as well as triumphs and accomplishments.

124. Easy is the twin of lazy.

125. Difficult is the cousin of determination.

126. Mediocre is the brother of excuse.

127. Success is the sister of effort.

128. Defeat is a setback. Retreat is a retrenchment. Only surrender is a failure.

129. Entrepreneurship depends on managing risk, not just taking it.

130. Pick your team to fly high and fly low.

131. There is a fine line between self-confidence and arrogance.

132. In the era of Big Data, how much of what we know do we understand?

133. If you're lucky enough to be an entrepreneur, then you're lucky enough.

134. Beware of the sense of entrepreneurial infallibility.

135. If necessity is the mother of invention then opportunity is the father of entrepreneurship.

136. Globalization rewards the small, flexible, and adaptable, focusing on economies of scale and the law of diminishing returns.

137. Entrepreneurs love the process, with the best part being you can do it again and again.

138. Focus on what you love while making sure you do the things that you hate.

139. In a quantum world there are no limitations.

140. Entrepreneurs define their world as quantum.

141. Entrepreneurship is an economic catalyst — the economic resource that puts all other resources to work.

142. Entrepreneurs love the process more than the project, the challenge more than the reward and the solution above all.

143. Opportunity is the father of entrepreneurship but determination is the cornerstone of success.

144. Entrepreneurship isn't a spectator sport. Teamwork is critical. The bench is thin. The coaches play.

145. If religion is the opiate of the masses, than optimism is the drug of choice for entrepreneurs.

146. Entrepreneurs exist in a revolving door of problem solving.

147. Don't neglect your most valuable asset. Pay yourself, take vacations, and find balance.

148. Indecision undermines leadership.

149. Being decisive inspires confidence.

150. Problems and complaints are the prime source of improvement.

151. Every problem is an opportunity. Every solution brings a reward.

152. Entrepreneurs are like the forwards in hockey: they dig in the corners and make things happen.

153. Every idea is not an opportunity. Every opportunity is not viable.

154. Entrepreneurs change the world and right now the world needs changing.

155. Entrepreneurship is a life philosophy sustained by determination.

156. Failure is not an essential part of being an entrepreneur. Failure sucks!

157. Fears are normal. Harness them to succeed.

158. One of the strongest motivations is the fear of failure.

159. The lean startup isn't new. Controlling costs and testing the market have always been prudent.

160. Fears are warnings helping you to anticipate. Embrace them to succeed. Deny them to fail.

161. Making sales at the expense of margin is like a dog chasing its tail. There is no fool like a busy fool.

162. We are a world in transition. Entrepreneurs must make contacts in emerging markets.

163. Park your ego. Trust your team. Being wrong happens. Admitting it does not make you weak.

164. A questioning mind is the source of many opportunities.

165. No one minds if you make a mistake. No one remembers once you fix it.

166. Entrepreneurs are jugglers, dealing with one thing but having several others on their radar.

167. Don't sacrifice your team culture through neglect.

168. People rarely change. If someone doesn't fit your team, every member knows it.

169. A career as an entrepreneur is like running the gauntlet. Everyone wants a piece of you but the run is glorious.

170. Life is an evolving path leading to opportunities but it takes a mind set to see them.

171. The most important skill you can master today is the ability to create and manage your own career.

172. The right people can make a bad idea a success.
173. The wrong people will make the best idea fail.
174. Disruption challenges the status quo, leading to innovation.
175. Entrepreneurs are disruptors.
176. It is creative destruction that renews capitalism.
177. Entrepreneurs are problem solvers. The bigger the problem, the bigger the reward.
178. We are entering a new age of entrepreneurship.
179. "Too big to fail" really means "too big to succeed."
180. Entrepreneurs have never been more important.
181. Every family business has a full cast of characters, both drivers and passengers.
182. Family loyalty can become an obsession, just one step away from delusion.
183. One of the principal barriers to entrepreneurship is prison thinking.
184. Family ties can literally bind you but family support can launch your success.
185. Simply being able to do something is a poor excuse for doing it.
186. The essence of consulting is finding multiple employers.
187. Creativity does not ensure viability.
188. The most painful result: becoming a creative success but a financial failure.
189. Technology is reducing the demand for labour.
190. Globalization is increasing the supply of available labour.
191. There is downward pressure on the price paid for labour in the form of real wages.
192. The middle class in the West is under downward pressure as real wages decline.
193. Job stability is disappearing in the face of global competition.
194. There is an increasing discrepancy in the distribution of wealth favouring the rich.
195. Employer expectations are increasingly focused on 24/7 availability.

196. Becoming an entrepreneur allows you to employ and capitalize on your own labour.

197. Becoming entrepreneurial allows you to manage and control your career.

198. Empathy is the key to understanding other's problems that lead to meaningful opportunities.

199. Family obligations can cloud judgement in the face of difficult decisions.

200. There will be thousands of independent businesses seeking successors within the next ten years.

201. The retirement plan for many baby boomers hinges on the sale of their business.

202. The marriage of a niche established businesses with up-to-date technology is a great opportunity.

203. There will soon be many businesses available that can be acquired on an earn-out basis.

204. Toxic relationships in a family business can sink a stable ship.

205. Never underestimate the determination and resilience of a CEO responsible for the family brand.

206. Life is not a dress rehearsal. Life is about self-determination.

207. There is no room for prison thinking in this new era of entrepreneurship.

208. The essence of being entrepreneurial is a mindset that does not allow us to fail.

209. It is never too early to start or too late to achieve.

210. Never underestimate the value of a critical eye from a seasoned veteran.

211. Self-determination beats waiting for a promotion, hands down.

212. It's one of life's little ironies that writers write because they don't like to speak.

213. Every individual needs to create his own brand.

214. Personal branding starts with entrepreneurial thinking and strategic decisions.

215. Free enterprise does not define entrepreneurship.

216. Free enterprise is just one environment in which entrepreneurs thrive.

217. Entrepreneurs will do well in any environment.

218. Entrepreneurship is an awkward word.

219. The perception of an entrepreneur is intimidating and surrounded with mystique.

220. Being an entrepreneur is about the results that you get not the risk that you take.

221. Risk should not be a barrier to entry whether in business or life itself.

222. Only one in ten venture capital projects succeed. The rest tank or go sideways.

223. Viability is a critical part of assessing any idea.

224. The ability to find a way within the quagmire of ever-expanding knowledge has become an essential skill.

225. There's a pressing need for mentorship from those who lived the life of an entrepreneur.

226. We are engaged in a continuous process of rebirth.

227. We need to educate new age renaissance men and women who can master change.

228. The middle class in under siege as the super-rich get richer.

229. We've reached an era where we have to trade in stability for agility.

230. Multi-nationals invest for profit maximization.

231. Entrepreneurs invest locally and are the key to solving structural unemployment.

232. Big corporations can't adjust fast enough.

233. Big business has to rely on acquisition and outsourcing to cope with change.

234. Acquisition and outsourcing create opportunities for individuals.

235. Tech is not the real world but it gets most of the attention.

236. Education is never a waste. It always increases opportunity.

237. Doing a personal SWOT analysis regularly is critical.

238. When we fail we know we have to change.

239. When we succeed we have a false sense of why.

240. Entrepreneurship depends on opportunity. Determination is not enough.

241. Governments need to remove barriers and then get out of the way.

242. There's a worldwide competition for entrepreneurial talent going on.

243. Finding a better way to serve a proven market reduces risk.

244. Positive thinking is critical. The power to make things happen is within us all.

245. Recognize the five stages of grief: denial, anger, bargaining, depression, and acceptance.

246. With youth comes passion, drive, and determination.

247. With age come experience and the ability to mentor.

248. If you stay in your comfort zone, nothing will change.

249. Three days is an eternity compared to some issues you're going to face.

250. Your differences can become your strength.

251. We're in the midst of an economic world in transition.

252. The limitation for seniors is resilience.

253. Are you more interested in methods or results?

254. We need to celebrate the successes of the *average*, not just billionaires.

255. Committed individuals can solve societal problems better and are less costly.

256. Doubts and fears are internal warnings that trigger closer examination.

257. They are the tools of defining managed risk as opposed to reckless risk.

258. Without doubt none of us would do downside planning leaving us less prepared.

259. If you keep waiting for the perfect opportunity, many others will pass you by.

260. Business succession offers a wealth of opportunities.

261. Individual initiative is a powerful force.

262. Don't over complicate it.

263. Opportunity is nowhere. Opportunity is everywhere.

264. Incubators provide a protected environment to shield entrepreneurs when they're most vulnerable: during the startup phase.

265. Every startup needs coaching on business fundamentals.

266. Success for an accelerator or incubator is measured in terms of equity created.

267. As an entrepreneur you will never work harder for less in the first year.

268. Business coaching has become a growth industry.

269. There is no better classroom than the business world.

270. There is no more willing student than the aspiring entrepreneur.

271. There is no proven method or system to teach entrepreneurship.

272. Sharing experiences with an effective mentor saves time and avoids mistakes.

273. Mentors build knowledge and prepare you.

274. Build and sell is a viable success strategy.

275. Much of the current tech dialogue revolves around scalability.

276. We are in an age of *corporatism* as opposed to capitalism.

277. The weight of responsibility is a burden.

278. Sales are the life's blood of viability.

279. Revenue generation is the foundation of success.

280. Crowdfunding is a critical development for the underfunded entrepreneurial world.

281. The only sure thing ahead of us is change.

282. Not all of us can be entrepreneurs. Every one of us can think like one.

APPENDIX II

Sam's Inspirations

When it comes to age and accomplishment, everyone has an opinion. Here are but a few that bring inspiration to the challenges dealt with in *Ageless Entrepreneur*:

"A society grows great when old men plant trees in whose shade they know they shall never sit."
— GREEK PROVERB

"Age appears to be best in four things: old wood best to burn, old wine to drink, old friends to trust, and old authors to read."
— FRANCIS BACON

"Aging is not lost youth but a new stage of opportunity and strength."
— BETTY FRIEDAN

"Forty is the old age of youth; fifty the youth of old age."
— VICTOR HUGO

"The most glorious moments in your life are not the so-called days of success, but rather those days, when out of dejection and despair, you feel rise in you a challenge to life, and the promise of future accomplishments."
— GUSTAVE FLAUBERT

"Even if it's absurd to think you can change things, it's even more absurd to believe that it is foolish and unimportant to try."
— PETER C. NEWMAN

"You can be young without money but you can't be old without it."
— ARISTOTLE

"If you live long enough, you'll make mistakes. But if you learn from them, you'll be a better person. It's how you handle adversity, not how it affects you. The main thing is never quit, never quit, never quit."
— WILLIAM JEFFERSON CLINTON

"The best time to plant a tree was twenty years ago. The second best time is now."
— CHINESE PROVERB

"Age is an issue of mind over matter. If you don't mind, it doesn't matter."
— MARK TWAIN

"The afternoon knows what the morning never suspected."
— ROBERT FROST

"To create an unbeatable combination, add the wisdom and experience of age to the relentless determination of youth."
— FRED DAWKINS

APPENDIX III

The Jargon of Entrepreneurship According to Sam

Accelerator: From the fast and furious world of technology and the venture capitalist determined to be the first to market comes the concept of the accelerator. They were established by early stage venture capital investors to speed up the process of converting new ventures to operating business. The measure of success is equity created, although much of it is of a speculative nature. The pressure to perform is intense. As Sam says this is not for everyone and a more cautious approach focused on managed risk works better in the traditional economy.

Becoming Your Own Brand: Managing and creating your own career means moving past the idea that *who you are* is partly determined by *where you work*. Job stability is gone. You will change positions several times during your work life. Making strategic decisions and developing marketable skill sets are critical for every individual. Whether this eventually translates into entrepreneurship or intrapreneurship is a personal choice, but blending in for stability is no longer a good option. Standing out for ability is the better choice. We are in the midst of trading in stability for agility and you need to embrace that reality.

Big Data: Sam often says that it's impossible to know everything. We are generating new knowledge at a phenomenal rate. Analytics is becoming the key to using knowledge. Collecting and analyzing information offers unlimited potential for new ventures. This trend is here to stay and will put increasing pressure on individuals to embrace change. Entrepreneurial thinking is the key to staying afloat in a world flooded with new thoughts and facts.

Bootstrapping: As a believer in self-determination, this is a concept that Sam loves since it depends on doing it yourself while living within your own means. It is slower and safer but far from conservative. The concept is grounded in proving viability and retaining equity rather than diluting yourself in a race to market. The mantra is managed risk. There is definitely a trade-off and as the pace of the world economy continues to accelerate there is a need for blending the two approaches even within the traditional economy.

Burn Rate: Definitely a bugbear for Sam, burn rate is tied to negative cash flow and it tells just how fast a startup venture is burning through its initial equity. Somehow the measure got a positive connotation from the tech world because it implies that the venture is attacking the market. For Sam the concept is linked to the misconception of entrepreneurship that focuses on reckless risk. It never ceases to amaze Sam that in seeking out investment a venture highlights the burn rate, which highlights when that venture will run out of money — not exactly negotiating from strength. For Sam this idea focuses the venture on raising capital, not investing it wisely, and it distracts from the more important goal of generating revenue.

Corporatism: In a world where large multi-national companies dominate the landscape of the global economy it is easy to conclude that capitalism is the dominant influence. Sam sees things quite differently. In a true capitalist world the individual has great opportunity. In a world dominated by huge corporations, individualism is suppressed while large firms control opportunity and markets and yield disproportionate returns to the super-rich. In our fast-paced world huge unwieldy corporations focused on controlling markets through branding have already proven ineffective, yielding up ideas like "too big to fail" as a rationale for the collective "we" to subsidize them. The public gets to help in the downside but the profits get distributed very selectively. It amounts to a perverse form of socialism that limits the opportunity and upward mobility of the individual. Entrepreneurship and entrepreneurial thinking are the best defence against unrestrained corporatism.

Crowdfunding: Sam knows this is an exciting new practice of funding a project or venture by raising investments/contributions from a large number of people, typically via the Internet. Lack of funds for entrepreneurs, especially outside the tech field, has become a significant limitation on our economic recovery. Entrepreneurs create jobs and they invest locally. Crowdfunding has the potential to solve the funding problem for small business finance and to provide individuals unique opportunities to invest. The best marriage is to raise funds from people who use and like your project combining fundraising with the lean startup idea of market feedback. It has tremendous potential if it doesn't become overregulated.

Disruptor: There is a theory that in order to create something new we must first destroy the prevailing alternative idea or product. Disruptors inherently challenge the status quo. Not all entrepreneurs are disruptors.

Entrepreneur: Sam defines entrepreneurs as problem solvers who make things happen. Most problems lead to opportunity — if you can solve problems you will find opportunity.

Incubator: The nature of an incubator is less intimidating. Sam believes that entrepreneurship can be taught. An incubator provides a safe haven where an inexperienced startup team can find mentorship, shared administrative services, inexpensive space and gain critical experience to make the transition from idea to a business. Unfortunately these facilities can become student ghettoes or comfort zones where ideas flounder and never make it to a viable business. Accelerators demand performance. Every incubator needs to incorporate benchmarks to ensure progress.

Intrapreneur: Being an intrapreneur is somewhat of an oxymoron in that it simply means acting like an entrepreneur while working within a large organization, whether a government or a large company. It's easier said than done within cultures that focus on systems and control at the expense of individual initiative. However in the current climate of relentless change challenging the status quo has become an asset that many entities are encouraging. As tough as this may seem there is opportunity on the rise for individuals who thrive on change as opposed to stability.

Lean Startup: Another Sam favourite and an idea that has gained a lot of attention in the tech community in the past few years. In reality it's been around as a business philosophy much longer. The approach is grounded in establishing viability through early market feedback as opposed to rushing a product to market in order to be first. The approach focuses on eliminating wasteful practices during the product development phase so that startups can have a better chance of success without requiring large amounts of outside funding. Customer feedback during product development is integral to the lean startup process, and ensures that the producer does not invest time designing features or services that consumers don't want. The foundation is practicing lean management (bootstrapping) until the product is proven. It is the antithesis of the approach inherent in the burn rate philosophy.

Mompreneur: For Sam one of the most critical elements that every entrepreneur needs to define for themselves is work/life balance. The decision is very subjective and should be. Mompreneurs are a special case defined as female business owners who are actively balancing the role of mom and the role of entrepreneur. Few people understand the power of social media networking better than mothers who, like all good entrepreneurs, have found the way to meet all their needs often by establishing online businesses they can conduct from home. It's no irony that "necessity" is considered the "mother" of invention. Entrepreneurship of necessity has become a major factor in our slowly recovering economy and stay-at-home moms have been in the forefront of finding solutions to their needs.

Scalability: A critical measure for venture capitalist but not for individual entrepreneurs. If build and sell is your plan it may be critical that your business can quickly evolve into a large entity with major market penetration but not everyone needs or wants investors, or a highly scalable business. Ninety percent of small businesses today are family businesses, which can be very successful, satisfying, and small by design. It's a strategic decision. Some entrepreneurs focus on growth above everything else. Others thrive on control and prefer medium sized manageable operations that they retain. There are many different types of entrepreneurs all of whom are valid and relevant.

Solopreneur: Entrepreneurs are often portrayed as consumed by growth. Sam believes that entrepreneurship is all about "self-determination" wherever that may lead you. Today with a laptop, cell phone, and a website an individual can run a very professional business based on a service that he or she can perform independently. In other words, it's very possible to become an entrepreneur who works alone, "solo," running their business single-handedly. They may have contractors that they hire, but they retain full responsibility for the running of their business. For these evolving types of entrepreneurs, independence supplants growth as the prime goal.